Second Edition

COLLECTOR'S GUIDE TO

EARLY PHOTOGRAPHS

O. HENRY MACE

Published by

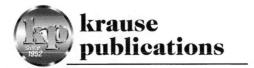

krause
publications

700 E. State Street • Iola, WI 54990-0001

Please call or write for our free catalog. Our toll-free number to place an order or obtain a free catalog is 800-258-0929 or please use our regular business telephone 715-445-2214 for editorial comment and further information.

Library of Congress Catalog Number: 89-51557
ISBN: 0-87341-720-8
Printed in the United States of America

ACKNOWLEDGMENTS

This book would never have been written without the encouragement and help of my wife Kathryn. In addition, my sincere thanks go to the following people who provided assistance in producing the second edition: Daile Kaplan and Caroline Birenbaum, Swann Galleries; and the following dealers and collectors whose images greatly enhance this work: Paul Berg, Tom Flood, Julie and Dominic Santangelo, Charles Schwartz, Joseph Silva, Terry Etherton, Charles Isaacs, Kathleen Fehr, Gregory Fried, D.J. Knowles, Jerry Mack, Cindy Motzenbecker, Randy New, and Richard and Gloria Schroeder.

Special thanks to John and Jelena McWilliams, and William Dunniway, for their contribution to this edition and their ongoing friendship and support.

CONTENTS

PREFACE

According to the old adage, a picture is worth a thousand words. Today, that picture could also be worth a thousand dollars, if it meets the proper criteria. In the case of early photographic images, "worth" is often a matter of opinion.

The people who collect nineteenth-century photographs are as diverse as the images themselves, and what is valuable to one collector may be worthless to another. This results in inconsistent and conflicting pricing, which can be quite confusing, especially to new collectors. The purpose of this book is to help both new and established collectors better understand factors which affect the value and collectibility of these early images.

It is important to note that nineteenth-century photographs are sold both as antiques and as art. It is no surprise that rare and premium examples almost always fit into the latter category, while common images are in the former. It is important to understand that early photographs have intrinsic or emotional value which can often affect their monetary worth. The personal appeal of an image to the collector is often a greater factor in the purchase decision than the image's rarity or price.

People who are interested in nineteenth-century photography are usually also interested in history. Often they view these early images as sort of a "time machine," giving them the ability to see the people, places, and events of another era, almost as if seeing them in person. To such people, to own an original image is to hold history in their hands.

Other collectors look at early photography with an artistic eye. They praise the use of light, composition, and posing in portraits, and the angles, depth, and shadow play in views. They extol the works of allegorical photographers and hold in reverence the members of the "Linked Ring" and the Photo-Secession group (see Glossary).

Still others see photography as a commodity, an investment whose value rises and falls with supply and demand. Such investors may or may not have any emotional attachment to an image, and it is probably best if they do not, for eventually it must be sold in order for the investor to realize a profit.

Regardless of why you collect early photographs, you will do well at it only if you are well-informed on the subject. The history and methodology of photographic processes have an important bearing on the collectibility and value of images. This book has been designed so that each major type of photography used during the nineteenth century has an individual chapter which includes a section concerning the history of the particular process, a section giving details of the process itself, and a section dealing with pricing trends and collectibility. The first read-through will provide you with a concise overview of nineteenth-century photography and current collecting trends. The guide can then be used as a convenient reference for identifying and evaluating acquisitions to your collection.

If you are a beginning collector, the information in this book will help you choose a specialty. Such a specialty might be a particular type of image, such as daguerreotypes, or a certain subject, such as landscapes. Your choice will be based mostly on personal emotional appeal, but careful consideration should be given to price and availability. For example, a collector who specializes in daguerreotype nude studies would have to be very diligent, patient, and wealthy.

The prices given in this book are based on documented recent sales and on a survey of current market trends. They are provided as the best method for collectors to compare relative values for particular types of images. The reader is regularly cautioned that value, like beauty, is in the eye of the beholder. Once you have ruled out that an image is a fake or a copy (to the best of your knowledge), then, using the information here as a guide, you should pay what the image is worth to you. Sometimes you will overpay, and sometimes you will get a bargain. If the image provides you with a degree of pleasure and satisfaction, it is worth the price you determine to be reasonable.

Investors, of course, should also base their decisions on comparisons to recent sales of similar pieces by well-known dealers and auction houses. Some examples are cited herein; however, sale catalogs are the bes source of this information.

The time span of nineteenth-century photography coincided almost exactly with an era named for Britain's Queen Victoria, who inspired a romantic style and an admiration for the finer things of life. Although the Victorians were staid and somewhat prudish, they developed a great appreciation for design, art, and architecture. Although their tastes were some-times somewhat garish, their homes were filled with the best of everything: silver, fine woods, leather, lace, and velvet. And, on nearly every table or shelf were the portraits of family and friends, albums filled with images of celebrities, travel scenes or art, and stereographs that could take the viewer to far-off lands or tell a funny story.

The Victorians were the first, and the best, photograph collectors, and for this we owe them our thanks. They have bequeathed to us the history of their era and the history of photography in its purest form. It is now up to us to protect and preserve that legacy.

AUTHOR'S PREFACE TO SECOND EDITION

When this collector's guide was first published nearly a decade ago, no one could have predicted the overwhelming surge in image collecting that has occurred during those ten years. The author flatters himself that he may have had some small influence by helping to inform the public of both the historical and investment value of early images. But one must also take into account the publicity generated by the sesquicentennial of the invention of photography in 1989, the extensive use of photography in popular public and commercial television documentaries, and a greater interest in historical subjects in general.

Veteran collectors like myself now look back to the '70s and '80s, berating ourselves for having turned down, as too expensive, images that are now bringing 10 or 20 times what we would have paid. The day when cased images could be found on flea market tables marked "old picture" has long passed (though uninformed sellers still cling to the unfortunate habit of marking all cased images as "daguerreotypes"–in various misspellings of the term). The layman may not know the correct name or how or even when the image was made, but for the most part, he or she is well aware that "old pictures" are valuable and sought after.

The preface to the first edition of this book describes three types of collectors–those who collect for the history, those who collect for the art, and those who collect for investment or gain.

In general, today's collector has a bit of all of these traits. There are still those who buy and sell early photographs strictly for profit. But for the most part, new collectors are drawn to the historical and aesthetic aspects of 19th century photography. The investment element is a bonus.

This revised collector's guide reflects the changes of the last decade in restoration and preservation, as well as collecting trends and values. It contains more than 250 new examples of collectable images from a variety of sources, many of which are published here for the first time. New appendices provide the collector with resource information for archival supplies, books, image clubs, and even the images themselves.

Collector's Guide to Early Photographs has introduced thousands to the joys and perils of image collecting over the past ten years. This new edition will spark thousands more to rummage through old trunks, scour flea market tables, and rifle through boxes of "instant relatives" in antique shops...in search of those little bits of time caught on metal, glass, or paper. Prices have risen, trends have changed, and far more people are involved in collecting than in 1989. But despite all the changes of the past decade, one thing remains the same: If you want to travel back in time, there is only one way to do it... by collecting and enjoying early photographs.

PART I

CASED IMAGES

Daguerreotypes,
Ambrotypes,
and Tintypes

1 8 3 9 - 1 8 6 9

CHAPTER 1

DAGUERREOTYPES

da 'guerre o type: Image produced on a silver-coated copper plate. Sensitizing agent: iodine, developing agent: mercury. Invented by Frenchman Louis-Jacque-Mande Daguerre

Introduced   1839
Peak years   1852-1854
Waned   1858-1860

Guide to Identification of the Daguerreotype

For the seasoned collector, daguerreotypes are perhaps the easiest of 19th-century images to identify. However, beginning collectors and many antique dealers often confuse daguerreotypes with later cased images: ambrotypes and tintypes. Daguerreotypes were made on a brightly polished silver plate; therefore, they exhibit a mirror-like quality. If you reflect a white piece of paper onto the surface of the "mirror," the image will appear as a negative. The daguerreotype is perhaps the most "brilliant" of early images, usually exhibiting a wide tonal range with rich blacks and bright whites as compared to usually "lackluster" ambrotypes and tintypes.

Fig. 1-1. Two Sisters, 1/4-plate daguerreotype.

From the very beginning, the typical daguerreotype portrait was one or more persons standing or sitting, facing the camera with their hands in their lap or with an arm leaning on a table, faces expressionless. This highly collectible daguerreotype is far from typical. (Collection of Gregory Fried)

The History of the Daguerreotype

It is interesting to note that although 1839 is generally considered the birth date of photography, cameras were used as early as 1544 to view the solar eclipse, and an instrument called the *camera obscura*, which projected an image onto paper for tracing, had been used by artists since the seventeenth century.

In 1827, Frenchman Joseph–Nicéphore Niépce used a camera obscura to produce the first semi-permanent photographic image, a view taken from the window of his home in Gras (the image, produced on a pewter plate, still exists in the Gernsheim Collection, Austin, Texas). Two years later, Niépce formed a partnership with Parisian artist Louis–Jacques Mandé Daguerre who, after Niépce's untimely death in 1833, succeeded in perfecting the world's first practical photographic process, called the *daguerreotype*.

The French government awarded Daguerre a yearly pension in exchange for the details of his process, which the government wished to reveal to the world as a gift of France. A manual, published in August of 1839, quickly made its way into the hands of scientists and artists around the world.

In Daguerre's home country of France, excitement over the new invention spread quickly. Early in 1840, publisher N. P. Lerebours commissioned a number of daguerreotypists to take views of important scenic and architectural attractions around the world. These beautiful daguerreotypes were then reproduced by engraving in a book called *Excursions Daguerriennes*.

A number of expeditions of this type were mounted throughout the 1840s and 1850s. Lerebours opened the first portrait studio in France in 1841 and also began production of photographic "art studies" (nudes).

Fig. 1-2. Le Camera Daguerre.

The Daguerre cameras, manufactured by Alphonse Giroux in Paris starting in 1839, were in great demand by scientists and others anxious to try the newly invented process. Early lenses were too slow for portraiture, prompting new designs from Voigtländer in Germany, among others. (Art by David White)

Frenchman Antoine Claudet, residing and working in England, introduced an acceleration process which shortened exposure times enough to make portraiture by the daguerreotype practical. Claudet and the major daguerreotypists of France displayed the best of their work at the French Product Exposition in 1844. The daguerreotypes of nearly 1,000 artists were exhibited.

Daguerreotypy reached its zenith in France around 1847. As the 1850s approached, the French were becoming better known for their expertise in producing photographic images on paper.

In Germany, Berlin businessman Louis Sachse was waiting for a shipment of daguerreotype equipment from Daguerre when he learned that, across town, optician Theodore Dorffel was already building and selling daguerreotype apparatus. This was only weeks after Daguerre's manual was published. While German daguerreotypes are not commonly available to collectors outside that country today, thousands were produced, for reproduction by engraving and by portrait artists and amateurs. Some of the

finest artistic portraits still in existence were taken by the Biow and Stelzner partnership of Hamburg (1842).

Perhaps the most important German contributions came in the form of improvements to daguerreotype apparatus. A superior portrait lens, developed by Josef Petzval and manufactured by Voigtländer, achieved immediate acclaim and was soon in demand by daguerreotypists around the world.

Fig. 1-3. California Gold Miner, 1/6-plate daguerreotype.

Both the California Gold Rush and Westward expansion were among the first major historical events to be captured by the daguerreotypists camera. Miners flocked to California operators to have their images made, either as a memento of their adventure or to send home to waiting wives and family. (Courtesy of Tom Flood)

The Daguerre cameras, produced in France and distributed by Alphonse Giroux, made their way to Italy in November of 1839. There, optician A. Duroni gave a public demonstration in the city of Milan. As in France and Germany, many Italian daguerreotypes were assembled for reproduction as engravings in books and travelogues. Some of the best of these were superb architectural and scenic views by Lorenzo Suscipj and Achille Morelli of Rome.

Fig. 1-4. Mother and Daughter, round daguerreotype.

The clothing styles of the sitters in this unusual piece suggest they may be Italian. The frame is made of elaborately carved wood. Framed daguerreotypes were far more common in Europe than in America, where all sizes were typically mounted in cases of the style used at the time for jewelry and delicate tools. (Courtesy of Charles Schwartz, Ltd.)

The daguerreotype was Daguerre's and France's gift to the world—with the exception of England. For reasons which invite speculation, Daguerre hired Miles Berry, as his agent, to apply for a British patent on the daguerreotype process. This made England the only country in the world which could not make use of the process free of charge. It is possible that Daguerre and France wanted to assert the precedence and superiority of this French invention over Talbot's calotype. Whatever the reason, the move severely hindered the growth of daguerreotypy in England.

Very few British amateurs were willing to pay the price of a license, and therefore British daguerreotypy was limited primarily to professional portraiture. The first two galleries to become well established were those of rivals Richard Beard and Antoine Claudet. Both Claudet and Beard were working on a bromide accelerator to shorten the necessary exposure times for portraiture. It was primarily through the efforts of Beard's associate, John Goddard, that this accelerator was perfected and Beard's studio opened in March of 1841.

Portraits were taken in the Beard gallery using the *speculum camera*, invented by Americans Alexander Wolcott and John Johnson. The design of this camera used a mirror instead of a lens, which afforded the increased speed required for portraiture. Wolcott and Johnson also helped to design an "operating room" setup which would become the pattern for a chain of Beard galleries throughout London. These galleries were the first to produce hand-colored daguerreotypes, many the work of the renowned Swiss painter J. B. Isenring. Early examples of these works, stamped "Beard patentee," today are rare and extremely valuable.

Despite the scale and success of Beard's establishments, his rival, Antoine Claudet, surpassed him in all areas. Claudet was instructed by Daguerre in 1839 and received the first English license in 1840. He provided daguerreotypes for the *Illustrated London News* and was the daguerreotypist of choice for celebrities in both England and France.

During the 1840s, Regent Street became the center of daguerreotypy in London. One of the most famous galleries there was that of John Mayall, who specialized in oversized portraits, illustrative views, and the first vignetted portraits (see "The Daguerreotype Process"). Mayall remained an active and influential proponent of photography throughout the nineteenth century. Also on Regent Street were William Kilburn, who used daguerreotypy to produce finely detailed miniature paintings, and William Telfer's Photographic Establishment, licensed in 1848. Operating in low-rent districts around London were a number of "black market" galleries that produced daguerreotypes without a license.

In England, as in France, the daguerreotype was quickly superseded by paper photography. Richard Beard was bankrupt in 1849 due to a court battle over patent rights, leaving Antoine Claudet as the last great daguerreotypist in England. Claudet remained active well into the 1850s specializing in stereo images.

While the English labored under stringent patent laws and the French basked in the exaltation of their ingenuity, Americans were quickly turning daguerreotypy into "big business."

Fig. 1-5. Lady in Bonnet, 1/4-plate daguerreotype.

This wonderful study in 1850's head wear is housed in a passe-partout frame. While this framing style was used occasionally in the U.S., it was more common in European countries. (Collection of the author)

Inventor Samuel Morse had visited Daguerre early in 1839, and when details of the daguerreotype process arrived in America aboard the steamer Great Western in September of that year, Morse and his associate John Draper began experimenting with portraiture, and teaching the process to others. New Yorkers Alexander Wolcott and John Johnson developed the specialized portrait camera mentioned earlier and opened a portrait studio in March of 1840, just six months after details of the process had been published. By 1841, hundreds of Americans were involved in the daguerreotype "industry."

Back in November of 1839, a Frenchman named Francois Gouraud had arrived in America as Daguerre's agent and apparatus distributor. Although his methods and motives were suspect, there is no doubt that Gouraud's lectures and demonstrations were paramount to the rapid proliferation of new daguerreotypists. Early in 1840, a Gouraud lecture was attended by a 29-year-old Bostonian named Albert Sands Southworth, who then immediately went to Professor Morse for instruction. Shortly thereafter, a partnership was formed between Southworth and Morse's assistant, Joseph Pennell. The two opened a studio in Cabotsville, Massachusetts, which was moved to Boston in 1841, at which time Pennell was replaced by J.J. Hawes. Inspired by Gouraud and taught by Morse, the team of Southworth and Hawes came to represent the best in early photographic documentation and portraiture. Today, hundreds of Southworth and Hawes daguerreotypes have found homes in museums nationwide, and still more await discovery and identification.

A less providential legacy was left by another famous American pioneer, John Plumbe. In 1838, he was employed by the U.S. government to investigate the possibility of a coast to coast,

east-west railroad link. When funds ran out in 1841, he took up daguerreotypy, opening 14 studios nationwide in just four years. He became one of the largest suppliers of apparatus and materials and was the first to attempt a "famous portraits" collection. He also developed hand-engraved daguerreotype copies which he called "plumbeotypes." Although a relatively large number of images bear John Plumbe's name, few of them were actually taken by him. Plumbe traveled extensively throughout the 1840s, still dedicated to the idea of a transcontinental railroad, and began selling off his galleries in 1847. When his railroad dream never materialized, he became deeply depressed and, in 1857, died by his own hand.

Plumbe had maintained a monopoly in Philadelphia until 1843 when German-born William and Frederick Langenheim appeared. As agents for Voigtländer cameras and Petzval lenses, their contribution to American daguerreotypy was solidly established. Later they would become major figures in the introduction of stereography, calotypy, and photography on glass.

Fig. 1-6. Brothers by John Plumbe, 1/6-plate daguerreotype.

Plumbe maintained a large chain of galleries and traveled extensively between them. Images that bear his name on the pad or mat were not necessarily taken by him, but more likely by one of his trained assistants. (Collection of Julie & Dominic Santangelo)

By the mid-1840s, every major city in America had several daguerreotype galleries. But it was in New York that the industry was shaped and refined. By 1850, there were nearly 100 galleries in that city, most of which were located on or near Broadway. The most famous of these was owned by Mathew Brady. No name in the history of photography evokes such interest–or such controversy.

Brady received instruction from Samuel Morse in 1844 and opened a very successful gallery across from the P.T. Barnum museum. During the early years, he received numerous awards, a trend which would continue throughout his long career. He recognized the publicity value of such awards, as well as the value of association with celebrities. It then became his ambition to make a photographic record of the famous and notable personages of his era, called the "Gallery of Illustrious Americans." Many photographs of important political figures of the nineteenth century would never have existed without the efforts of Mathew Brady.

Although many historical images bear the Brady name, it is unknown how many were actually taken by him. He employed many operators throughout his career, all of whom were trained to the Brady system. Perhaps as much as 75 percent of the total volume of images bearing the name Brady were actually taken by these trained operators. However, this in no way lessens his importance as an innovator, teacher, and entrepreneur or his position as America's most valuable photo historian. Mathew Brady's involvement in the photographic field was so immense that you will find reference to him in nearly every chapter of every book on the early history of photography.

While Brady was the most famous of the New York daguerreotypists, he was not without important competition. The Broadway galleries of Jeremiah Gurney and Martin Lawrence were equally as active, and both Gurney and Lawrence were recipients of numerous major awards for daguerreotype excellence.

Other well-known American daguerreotypists included Abraham Bogardus, Rufus Anson, Samuel Broadbent, C. D. Fredricks, and the Meade Brothers, all in New York City; Marcus

Fig. 1-7. Men with Top Hats, 1/4-plate daguerreotype.

In a deviation from the posing "norm," the operator had these two dapper gentlemen stand and hold their top hats in their hand. The relatively long exposure times required that the sitters remain as motionless as possible, thus the "stiff" countenance. (Collection of William Dunniway)

Root in Philadelphia; John Whipple in Boston; John Fitzgibbon in St. Louis; and Robert Vance and the Shew brothers in California. During the early 1850s, some galleries began using the production line concept to produce portraits for as little as 25 cents each for 1/9-plate images. Brady and the other top galleries condemned these "cheap pictures" and lashed out at the operators who advertised them. However, history has shown that some of these daguerreotypes were as good or better than many taken by elaborate and expensive establishments.

Fig. 1-8. Daughter with Parents, 1/4-plate daguerreotype.

The operator has arranged these family members in a classic triangular pose established before the invention of photography by artists. In the original image, the daughter's clothing is fully tinted, while the parents remain black and white. Note eye-glasses in mother's hand. (Collection of D. J. Knowles)

Even as the rest of the world began to concentrate on paper photography, American daguerreotypy flourished. Major cities were overrun with galleries, while itinerants carried the process to small frontier towns and even to California. The first Western routing expeditions and the gold rush were all documented by the daguerreotype. In 1853, daguerreotypists were enjoying the overwhelming success of their chosen profession, unaware that in just a few short years, the silver-coated plate would be replaced by collodion on glass (see Chapter 6) and the world's first practical form of photography would soon become obsolete.

The Daguerreotype Process

Daguerre had experimented with numerous other materials before finally arriving at the choice of a silver-coated copper plate as the base of his process. He used the recently invented electroplating system to "galvanize" silver onto the copper surface, and then the plate was given an acid wash to remove impurities. The plate was next placed in a closed box where it was subjected to iodine vapors. Now sensitized, it was exposed in a camera of Daguerre's design. In Daguerre's early experiments, exposures could take as long as 30 minutes and averaged no less than 5 minutes. After exposure, the plate was placed in a second box where, by the fumes of heated mercury, the latent image was developed. A finishing bath in hyposulfate of soda ("hypo") made the image permanent.

Fig. 1-9. Clean-cut Man by J. P. Ball, 1/6-plate daguerreotype.

James Ball was a rare black daguerreotypist who operated in Cincinnati, Ohio from 1845. The posing in this wonderfully sharp image is the classic arm-on-table arrangement used to give a more relaxed look and to help stabilize the sitter. (Collection of D. J. Knowles)

The process sounded simple, but early practitioners discovered that great patience and attentiveness were required to obtain acceptable results. After Daguerre's manual, *Historiqué et Description des Procédés du Daguerréotype et du Diorama*, was published in 1839, experiments were soon undertaken to improve the process. England's John Goddard found that by including bromide in the sensitizing process the sensitivity could be greatly increased. Eventually, individ-ual operators would devise their own secret sensitivity–increasing formulas, called "quickstuff." These "quicks," along with other improvements, such as Wolcott and Johnson's speculum camera, made commercial daguerreotype portraiture a reality.

By the late 1840s, the process had been generally standardized. Plates were purchased from silversmiths who brazed silver sheets onto copper. Often the individual operators would then galvanize additional silver to the plate through electrolysis. A wet battery served as a source for the electroplating current. In 1851, the French platemaker Christofle began selling factory-galvanized plates, thus eliminating one of the time-consuming operations.

Before use, each plate had to be polished to a mirror-like finish. It was attached to a holder, which sometimes required bending or gluing, then buffed, first with a leather-covered "buffing stick" and pumice and then with flannel cloth and jeweler's rouge. Since even the most thorough buffing left tiny scratches, the final strokes had to be performed so that these buff marks were parallel to the intended viewing light (lengthwise for horizontal format images and side to side for vertical format images). An 1849 manual suggested that buffing be done immediately before sensitizing, when the plate was still warm.

In large establishments, each part in the process was performed by a separate department with workers who specialized in a particular step or function. In such an establishment polishing was often done on a large steam-powered buffing machine. The plate was then taken to the "coating room," where it was sensitized, first in an iodine coating box and then with quickstuff, before being placed in a shield for delivery to the waiting camera operator. All of this took place as the customer was led from the lounge to the "operating room" and posed before the camera.

Fig. 1-10. Smiling Woman, 1/6-plate daguerreotype.

It was once said that the reason people did not smile for daguerreotype portraits was because they could not hold a smile for the long exposure. Exposure times during the heyday of daguerreotypy were only a few seconds, but the process of having your image made was a serious matter to most. Accordingly, daguerreotypes of smiling people are uncommon and prized by collectors. (Collection of Gregory Fried)

There have been numerous horror stories told about the discomforts involved in sitting for a daguerreotype portrait. It has become apparent that the degree of comfort experienced by the sitter was directly proportional to the degree of care and patience provided by the operator. The primary "evil" in these horror stories was the "head rest," a U-shaped device attached to the chair or a heavy metal stand, designed to keep the head motionless during exposure. When used properly, the head rest was just that–a rest on which to lean the head. In most cases, the pained looks and grim expressions are not signs of discomfort, but signs of the time.

With the head rest in place and the sitter posed, the operator received a freshly sensitized, shielded plate which he or she then slipped into the camera. The slide covering the plate was removed, the lens uncapped, and the exposure made. (Many operators would recite poems or sayings as a way of measuring the exposure times.) Then the cap and slide were replaced and the exposed plate removed to the developing room.

In semi-darkness, the plate was taken from the shield to a mercury fuming box in which the latent image would be brought out. Careful control of time and temperature was necessary in this step. After development, the image was made permanent in a fixing solution of hyposulfate of soda. Next, the plate received a toning bath in gold chloride. This "gilding" process improved the tone of the image and also provided protective elements.

Fig. 1-11, 1-12, 1-13. The Absent Master, 1/6-plate daguerreotype.

One wonders whether it was the operator or sitter who came up with this poignant arrangement. A woman sits solemnly next to a chair and headrest. From the headrest dangles a locket containing the image of a man...an absent husband or son, and most likely the master of the dog who occupies the chair. An exceptional story-telling daguerreotype. (Collection of William Dunniway)

After the plate was washed and dried, several finishing steps could be performed. Most galleries employed artists who applied varying degrees of color in the form of powdered pigment. When elaborate coloring was required, stencils were cut to isolate the area receiving a particular color. In America, finished daguerreotypes were then taped to a cover glass with a decorative (and protective) brass mat sandwiched between. The packet was then placed in a leather, papier-mâché, or plastic case (see Chapter 4). In France and other European countries, the daguerreotype was often displayed behind painted glass and cardboard frames called *passe-partout* (detailed later in this chapter). The various elements which protect and adorn the daguerreotype add considerably to the enjoyment of collecting these images. By careful study of these various elements, collectors can often arrive at an approximate date for the image, as well as determine other interesting facts about its production.

The Daguerreotype Plate

Most plates were purchased from distributors, who purchased them from plate manufacturers. These manufacturers employed silversmiths who brazed a block of pure silver to a larger block of copper, rolling the combination out until the proper thickness was reached. On the finished sheet (only .02 inches thick), the silver layer was a mere 3 percent of the total weight. (When silver commanded its highest price during the 1970s, enterprising individuals who attempted to extract the silver by melting daguerreotype plates quickly found that it wasn't worth the effort.) This large sheet was cut into standard-sized plates which were then stamped with the manufacturer's hallmark.

Historians and writers seem to disagree as to the exact dimensions of these standard plates, probably because the two primary sources of this information (early catalogs and existing plates) are inconsistent. Measurement controls in factories were not always accurate, and more often than not the plates required additional trimming by the daguerreotypist. The list provided below is based on average measurements taken from this author's collection:

Full plate	6-1/2" x 8-1/2"
Half plate	4-1/2" x 5-1/2"
1/4 plate	3-1/8" x 4-1/8"
1/6 plate	2-5/8" x 3-1/4"
1/9 plate	2" x 2-1/2"
1/16 plate	1-3/8" x 1-5/8"

These sizes carried over into all types of cased images. I have also found references to a 1/8" plate (2-1/8" x 3-3/4") and plates as large as 20" x 24".

Although American daguerreotypists were considered the best in the world, it was the French who produced the best daguerreotype plates. The most widely used French plates bore the initials H. B. or the initials J. P. in their hallmarks. The actual names of these manufacturers have not been determined.

Hallmark designs usually consisted of a star or initials, followed by a symbol (eagles, scales, horses, etc.) and a number which indicated the ratio of silver to copper. Commonly this number was 40, indicating 1 part silver to 39 parts copper. High-quality plates marked "20" and "30" and inferior quality plates marked "60" were rarely used. In England and America, the plate mark often consisted only of the manufacturer's name stamped on an edge or corner (see Appendix B).

These hallmarks are an important aid in dating a daguerreotype image, since manufacturers often changed the designs to indicate changes in process, quality, or ownership.

Unfortunately for the collector, many operators·bought full plates which they then cut into various sizes, as needed. The hallmark would then only appear on one of these "self-cut" plates.

The quality of the original plate played an important part in the overall results of the daguerreotype process. Only a well-polished plate, galvanized and properly sensitized, could produce a superior daguerreotype. One of the most difficult parts of the polishing operation was to keep the plate still during the aggressive buffing process. A number of devices were designed and patented during the late 1840s and early 1850s to hold the plate firmly in place. The various marks (bent corners or edges, indentations) left by these plate holders can be used as an aid in image dating. Plates with holder marks can be positively attributed to the period after 1848.

Fig. 1-14. A Guide to Daguerreotype-plate sizes.

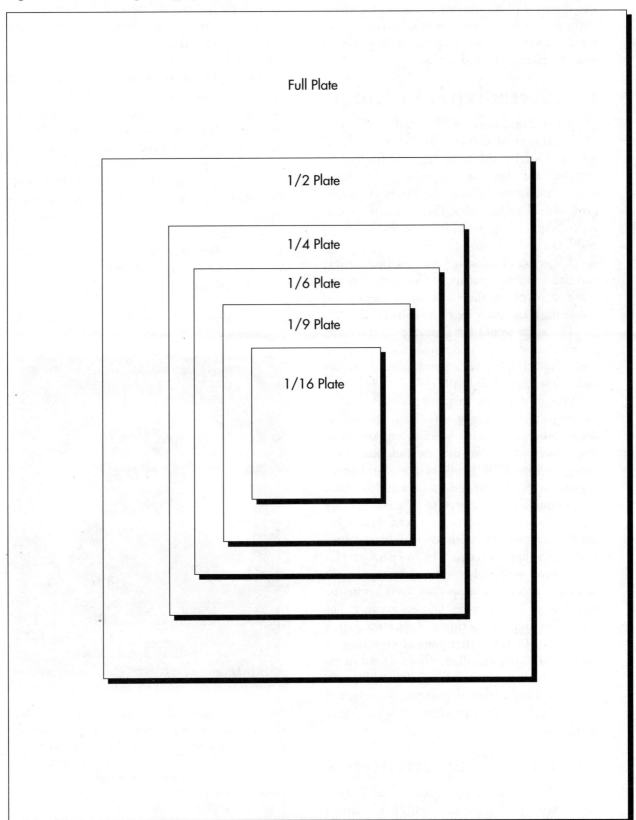

However, not everyone used these devices, and therefore plates without marks are not necessarily pre-1849. During the mid-to-late 1840s, some daguerreotypists used red sealing wax to hold the plate to a wooden block.

Daguerreotypes in Color

Most daguerreotype portraits had some small amount of coloring added by artificial means. Usually this coloring was limited to "pinking" the cheeks and applying gilt to chains or jewelry; however, some operators employed professional artists who, through careful and expert application, could color an entire image with amazingly true-to-life results.

A number of coloring processes, both simple and elaborate, were patented. The most common method involved the creation of stencils to isolate the areas receiving a particular color.

The artist would then breathe on the plate, forming condensation to which the pigmented dust would cling. Other artists applied the colors with a fine camel-hair brush.

One of the most fascinating stories of early photographic history involves the color daguerreotypes of Levi L. Hill, an American daguerreotypist residing in New York during the early 1850s. Hill produced a number of daguerreotypes in the "colors of nature," which were examined and attested to by contemporary experts. Existing examples have been thoroughly studied by modern methods which reveal no evidence of applied color. "Hillotypes," as Hill called them, were truly produced by the world's first color process, developed 85 years before the invention of Kodachrome. Unfortunately, Hillotypes were simply an accident of chemical experimentation. In 1865, after years of promising to divulge his secret, Hill died, still frustrated in his attempts to recreate the chemical combination. In recent years, modern daguerreotypists claimed to have duplicated the process with some degree of success.

Vignetted Daguerreotypes

In 1849, John Whipple patented the "crayon daguerreotype," a process which produced vignetted portraits with a light-colored background. By keeping the dark or shadow areas to a minimum, the crayon portrait greatly reduced the annoying reflections which had been the daguerreotype's greatest drawback.

During the 1850s, a number of variations of vignetted daguerreotypes were introduced. The two most popular were the "magic background" and the "illuminated daguerreotype." In the magic background process, a series of paper cutouts were placed over the center of the plate during the exposure to produce a halo around the subject. Illuminated daguerreotypes were similar to crayon portraits but were produced through manipulation of the mercurializing process, allowing the outer edges of the plate to receive less mercury and thus producing the effect of light coming from behind the subject.

Fig. 1-15. Vignetted Girl with Ringlets, 1/6-plate daguerreotype.

Operators employed a wide variety of methods to produce vignetted portraits. At first glance, this image would appear to be a copy of a daguerreotype in an oval mat. However, the halo surrounding the opening indicates the operator held an oval mat in front of the camera to produce this special effect. (Collection of D. J. Knowles)

Considering the simplicity of the process and the beauty of the resulting images, it is surprising that more crayon daguerreotypes were not produced. It may have been that the restrictions imposed by Whipple's patent or the licensing requirements of Whipple's agent Marcus Root kept the process from being used extensively.

Mats and Preservers

The purpose of brass mats, which lay between a daguerreotype plate and its coverglass, was twofold: first, to frame and enhance the image, and second, to provide a protective space between the image and the glass. Because the style and texture of these mats changed over the years, they provide today's collector with a quick reference indicating the approximate year an image was made.

Early mats were relatively thick and unadorned, becoming slightly more ornate around 1850 and then more lightweight and elaborate after 1855. Occasionally mats were embossed with the gallery name and address. When daguerreo-

types were placed in jewelry, or in round or oval cases in which a mat was not feasible, a convex glass was sometimes used to provide the protective separation.

During the early years (1839 to 1845), a full sheet of paper was often glued to the back of the plate and wrapped over the edges of the cover-glass to hold all the elements together. Later, a small strip of paper or thin tape, of the type used by goldbeaters in the production of gold-leaf, was employed for the purpose. Around 1849, a thin frame of malleable brass was introduced which slipped over the cover glass and wrapped around the back of the plate. This frame, called a *preserver*, was at first straight and narrow, embossed with simple patterns. After 1855, preservers were much lighter in weight and more ornate.

On the Continent, Europeans usually preferred to have their daguerreotypes mounted in frames of the type called *passe-partout*. For passe-partout frames, a cardboard mat was cut and pressed to provide an oval or double elliptical opening edged in gold, black, or white. The plate and mat were then taped to a cover-glass, which may have been lacquered in black or painted to resemble tortoiseshell or marble.

The British also used both the passe–partout style frame or a leather case similar to those used in the United States, but with either a plain leather cover or embossed with the Royal Seal.

Understanding the many elaborate steps involved in the making of a daguerreotype should give the collector a greater appreciation for the end product. Today, only a handful of people are capable of producing a quality example, yet during the period of the daguerreotype's popularity, more than 25 million were produced by amateurs and professionals around the world. Perhaps most remarkable were the itinerants who worked in small wagons and tents on muddy back roads and snow-covered mountainsides.

Fig. 1-16. Three Sisters, 1/4-plate daguerreotype.

A wonderful study of three young Victorian ladies, this image shows the open-necked dresses normally worn by young girls as well as the classic long ringlet curls in style during the early 1850s. Collectors should familiarize themselves with period clothing and hairstyles as an aid in dating images. (Collection of Gregory Fried)

The profession of daguerreotypy was risky in many ways, for the process involved poisonous chemicals, sharp edges, and one of the most dangerous elements of the nineteenth century–fire. Hundreds of photographic establishments were destroyed by fire, often taking the entire town with them. Many important images were also lost when the buildings in which they were stored or displayed were lost to fire.

The daguerreotype was the first, most permanent, most difficult, and in the opinion of many afficionados, the most beautiful of photographic processes. For this reason alone, existing examples can only become more valuable in the years to come.

Collecting the Daguerreotype

Even though the reign of the daguerreotype was somewhat short (1839-1860), this area of photographic history today provides a wide range of appeal for both collectors and investors.

Interesting portraits can be found at flea markets and antique shops for less than $50. At

Fig. 1-17. Man with Fiddle, 1/6-plate daguerreotype.

Daguerreotypes containing musical instruments are uncommon and prized by collectors. (Courtesy of Charles Schwartz, Ltd.)

the same time, record prices in excess of $75,000 have been paid for individual examples at auction.

Collectors are drawn to the historic and aesthetic appeal of the daguerreotype. As the first commercially marketable form of photography, its wide success assured generous stockpiles for future collectors. While unique examples are becoming harder to find, the stockpile is far from empty.

Fig. 1-18. Captain William Chapman and Friend at Vera Cruz, 1/4-plate daguerreotype.

Shortly after he purchased this image, the owner began backtracking its origin and located the descendants of the sitter, obtaining considerable biographical background. A unique and wonderful daguerreotype such as this has considerable value even if the subjects are unknown. By taking the time and effort to document the associated whos, whats and wheres, the collector has made the image virtually priceless. (Collection of William Dunniway)

From a historic point of view, the daguerreotype is a "mirror of the past." Reflecting, in bold sharpness, the visage of America's pioneers, its recording quality is unrivaled. From an aesthetic point of view, this silver plate in a golden frame, housed in a rich leather case trimmed in velvet, is definitively Victorian. It is showy, yet classy. It is stylish and romantic. It is no surprise that organizations dedicated to this one unique nineteenth-century photographic process have been formed around the world.

Daguerreotypes in all price ranges have more than doubled in value during the past decade. Common examples that were found on flea market tables for $20 to $30 just a few years ago are now going for $60 and up. Once just an "old picture in a leather case," the "secret" of the daguerreotype as a valuable and artistic historical record has been revealed.

What to look for

Daguerreotypes which in any way stand out from the thousands of common images on the market are collectible pieces, highly subject to value appreciation. A seemingly common portrait can actually be uncommon when the sitter is identified as a famous statesman or author, or when the image is found to bear a rare plate hallmark. While most images purchased from secondary sources (dealers, auction houses) have usually been thoroughly studied, the well-educated collector can often discover a hidden treasure, especially when dealing with original and "first purchase" owners.

Whenever possible, try to ascertain the provenance of a piece (see Glossary). This is especially important when buying rare and premium examples, since a list of successive owners usually confirms the authenticity of the work and the legality of the sale.

When contemplating a daguerreotype purchase, ask yourself the following three questions:

1. *Is the image content unusual?* In portraits, look for unusual clothing or uniforms, animals (cat in lap, dog on floor), and/or unusual backdrops or lighting; in common images, look for pipes, cigars, hats, canes, etc., which increase the collectibility of the image. Very early portraits often exhibit distortion, especially in the arms and fingers of the sitter and, if produced prior to 1843, are quite valuable. Some images stand out simply because of the artistic quality achieved through lighting and posing.

Fig. 1-19. The Outdoorsman, 1/6-plate daguerreotype.

For obvious reasons, images in which the sitter is wearing winter or outdoor clothing are unusual, and often relates to their occupation. This rugged fellow is probably a frontiersman, possibly a hunter, trapper, or guide. (Collection of Randy New)

2. *What is the condition of the piece?* Never buy a daguerreotype which requires major restoration, unless it is a bargain. Restoration reduces the value of a piece and causes irreparable damage. The aesthetics of age—worn cases and stained mats are in the eye of the beholder. For the most part, the image is what the collector should be concerned with, and a single scratch on a daguerreotype can lessen its value. With each additional scratch, the value continues to drop. Examine dust and condensation carefully. Dust or condensation on the glass can be cleaned; if they are on the plate, they could be trouble. Also remember that images with the original seal intact are more valuable.

3. *Is the price right?* A collector who is well versed in his or her subject can estimate the value of a piece after a basic examination. If the asking price is 10 to 20 percent below the value, it is often called a "buy"; if it is 30 to 40 percent lower, it is a "bargain." Never pass up a bargain! Under ideal circumstances, a purchase should be based on the following factors:

Rarity	20%
Aesthetics	20%
Condition	20%
Price	30%
Emotional appeal	10%

Of course, the ideal is rarely the case. Emotional appeal is frequently the largest factor in a purchase, especially among collectors. If you are assembling a collection for your own appreciation, without particular investment concerns, this reliance on emotional appeal is not necessarily a problem.

Availability/Value Classifications

The common daguerreotype ($30 to $100)

About 50 percent of the daguerreotypes on the market can be considered *common*. These are the ordinary portraits most often found at flea markets and in antique shops, or purchased from photograph dealers. An average 1/9-plate portrait usually sells for around $30 to $50. Common 1/6-plate portraits usually bring $35-$60. Slightly more valuable are those images containing children, flowers, hats, canes, spectacles, other cased images, and identified sitters ($50 to $100). Larger, 1/4-plate images will often bring $75-$100 or more, and tiny 1/16 plates bring $40 to $80 or more. If an image is in a good, complete case, the value is increased slightly ($5 to $10 additional). Common images in good Union Cases are usually much higher—see Uncommon Daguerreotypes. Scratched, buffed, or heavily tarnished images are considerably less valuable, though they may not be priced accordingly.

Examples of recent sales:

1/9 plate, ordinary portrait of young man, antique shop, $30

1/6 plate, portrait of young man, antique shop, $37

Fig. 1-20. Girl with Ringlet Curls, 1/6-plate daguerreotype.

Fig. 1-21. Woman with Spitcurls, 1/6-plate daguerreotype.

A properly made daguerreotype is the most detailed and accurate historical document available to historians. Nearly grainless and capable of superior recording qualities—the details of hair, clothing, and facial features of people who lived nearly 150 years ago are vividly and factually portrayed. (Collection of Gregory Fried)

1/6 plate, ordinary portrait of older man, antique shop, $42

1/9 plate, portrait of elderly woman with glasses, catalog, $45

1/6 plate, nicely posed portrait of pretty young woman, antique shop, $55

1/9 plate, daguerreotype copy of daguerreotype portrait, antique shop, $65

1/6 plate, nicely tinted portrait of seated girl, catalog, $65

1/6 plate, portrait of twin girls, catalog, $75

1/9 plate, ordinary portrait by Chase (imprint), antique shop, $75

1/6 plate, portrait of man with cane, antique shop, $75

1/16 plate, slightly blurred portrait of baby, antique shop, $85

1/6 plate, family group of four, catalog, $100

The uncommon daguerreotype ($100 to $1,000)

Uncommon images make up about 40 percent of the available daguerreotype base. They can occasionally be found in antique stores, but they are most often made available through dealers. Many of the images now classified as *uncommon* will easily slip into the *rare* category in the next few years, making them excellent investments now. On the lower end, portraits by identified photographers, postmortems (death portraits), painted backdrops, vignetted portraits, and ordinary 1/2-plate images are *uncommon*. On the upper end are occupational portraits, works by well-known daguerreotypists, images containing musical instruments, tools, or weapons, portraits of "known" individuals, lesser outdoor subjects, history-related, and copies of artwork—all of which may fit into either the *uncommon* or *rare* categories depending on the quality or uniqueness of the image. Images contained in unbroken Union cases (see Glossary) are also uncommon. Some images of seemingly ordinary subjects or poses may be categorized as uncommon due to exceptional posing, lighting, etc.

Examples of recent sales:

1/6 plate, well-dressed man holding rifle, auction, $977

1/2 plate, nice portrait of couple (also three 1/6 plates), auction, $747 lot

Fig. 1-22. Boy with Toy Gun, 1/6-plate daguerreotype.

(Collection of Gregory Fried)

1/4 plate, 2 nice portraits of couple in double Union case, antique shop, $600

1/6 plate, heavily scratched view of unknown building, dealer, $475

1/4 plate, damaged portrait of dog on posing table, auction, $450

1/6 plate, postmortem of young girl, auction, $402

1/4 plate, two girls looking at book by S. Broadbent, auction, $375

1/6 plate, occupational of man holding tools, dealer, $325

1/6 plate, sharp portrait of seated man with top hat and cigar, auction, $287

1/2 plate, nice portrait of two young boys, catalog $275

1/4 plate, five boys around table, framed image, auction, $258

1/4 plate, clear portrait of young man in nice Union Case, antique store, $225

1/6 plate, exceptional portrait of young girl with baby, catalog, $225

1/6 plate, heavily buffed (scratched) image of two-story white house, dealer, $200

1/6 plate, two daguerreotype copies of paintings, auction, $200 lot

1/6 plate, ordinary portrait by Plumbe (imprint), antique shop, $165

1/16 plate, portrait of handsome man in western hat, antique shop, $150

1/6 plate, nice portrait of young girl in near-mint Union Case, antique shop, $150

1/4 plate, portrait of couple by E. Long, auction, $150

1/6 plate, ordinary portrait by Pollock, auction, $125

1/16 plate, clear portrait of baby (mom's hand visible), antique shop, $100

Fig. 1-23. Identically Dressed Brothers, 1/6-plate daguerreotype.

Images of children are particularly popular with collectors. Clothing, toys, or other features of the image that make it unusual add to the collectibility. (Courtesy of Kathleen Fehr)

The rare daguerreotype ($1,000 to $5,000)

Rare daguerreotypes comprise less than 10 percent of all existing images. Most of these are offered through dealers or auctions. *Rare* daguerreotypes also include outdoor views; animal portraits; blacks and Indians; history-related; unusual half-plate, full-plate, and stereograph images; and certain works by well-known daguerreotypists. Collectors

Fig. 1-24. Daguerreotype Ring.

Photographic jewelry has been popular since the beginning of the art of photography. Daguerreotypes and later image types were placed in bracelets, lockets, watches, and rings. This ladies ring contains the image of an older woman in a day cap, likely the owner's mother or grandmother. This piece sold at auction in 1998 for $1,495.
(Courtesy of Swann Galleries, Inc.)

interested in this category should subscribe to dealer and auction catalogs and keep regular contact with those who deal in *rare* images. Some images are categorized as rare simply because of their superior and/or unique aesthetic qualities.

Examples of recent sales:

1/6 plate, sharp portrait of fireman with hat and horn, auction, $3,000

1/4 plate, girl riding hobby horse, auction, $1,840

1/6 plate, young girl with fluffy dog on lap, auction, $1,250

half plate, exceptional portrait of a couple by Fitzgibbon, auction, $1,150

Fig. 1-25. Postmortem of Young Girl, 1/6-plate daguerreotype.

Postmortem images–photographs of deceased individuals–are highly sought after by collectors. This image sold at auction in 1998 for $402. (Courtesy of Swann Galleries, Inc.)

half plate, nice portrait of couple in near-mint
Union case, antique shop, $1,000
half plate, nice group portrait of eleven identified
family members, dealer, $1,000

The premium daguerreotype ($5,000 and up)

In the average year, perhaps 10 individual *premium* daguerreotypes will come to auction or exchange hands via private sale. Generally, these are half-plate or full-plate images of scenic or architectural views, portraits of important historical figures, or documentary images of historic events.

The Future of Daguerreotype Collecting

During the past decade, prices of many daguerreotypes have doubled while others have as much as quadrupled. Heightened demand and a gradual decrease in the available base will continue to drive prices higher in the coming years. As of this writing, nice examples can still occasionally be found at antique shops and flea markets at reasonable prices. However, the collector will soon see a day when quality examples are seldom found outside photo shows and auction catalogs.

Fig. 1-28. Dark-skinned Young Girl, 1/9-plate daguerreotype.

Fig. 1-26. Portrait of a Black Man, 1/9-plate daguerreotype.

(Collection of D. J. Knowles)

The end of the daguerreotype era preceded the Civil War by only a few years. This was a time when African-Americans were either held as slaves or had achieved freedom through escape or by earning their release. Accordingly, very few were photographed, and those who appear dressed in quality clothing are very likely free blacks. Images such as these and fig. 1-27 on p. 35 are important historical documents and are prized by collectors. (Collection of D.J. Knowles)

Fig. 1-27. Black Girl in Pink Dress by Tyler & Co., 1/9-plate daguerreotype.

(Collection of D. J. Knowles)

Fig. 1-29. Portrait of a Couple, 1/6-plate daguerreotype.

At first glance, a collector might pass up this image as an ordinary portrait of a man and a woman. A closer look reveals the woman appears to be of African origins. Portraits of inter-racial couples are extremely rare historical documents.
(Collection of Joseph T. Silva)

Fig. 1-30. Copy of image sitting on books, 1/9-plate daguerreotype.

Fig. 1-31. Copy of image showing nail, 1/6-plate daguerreotype.

(Collection of Kathleen Fehr)

(Collection of the author)

Because daguerreotypes were one-of-a-kind images, copies had to be made by re-photographing the original. Although devices had been invented to make this process easier, many operators simply nailed the original to a board or sat it on any available support, such as a stack of books, as shown in these examples.

Fig. 1-32 Hunter, Dog, and Rabbit, 1/6-plate daguerreotype.

An extremely unusual studio portrait of a man holding a rifle, his faithful hunting dog at his feet and their latest "conquest" lying nearby, this is a daguerreotype that collector's dreams are made of.
(Collection of D. J. Knowles)

Fig. 1-33. Copy Portrait of Beautiful Girl, half-plate daguerreotype.

Prior to the invention of photography in 1839, portraits were made by the artist's hand—either paintings or drawings. Having these pictures copied as daguerreotypes made them more permanent and portable. (Collection of the author)

CHAPTER 2

AMBROTYPES and TINTYPES

'am bro type: Negative image produced on a glass plate, viewed as positive by the addition of a black backing. Sensitizing agent: silver nitrate; developing agent: pyrogallic acid. Invented by Frederick Scott Archer (Britain) and popularized by James Cutting (United States).

Introduced   1854   Peak years   1857-1859   Waned   1861-1865

'tin type (also called *melainotype* and *ferrotype*): Negative image produced on a thin iron plate, viewed as positive due to undercoating of black Japan varnish. Sensitizing agent: silver nitrate; developing agent: pyrogallic acid. Invented by Hamilton Smith. Patented by Peter Neff (United States).

Introduced   1856   Peak years   1860-1863   Waned   1865-1867

The last tintypes to be contained in cases were produced around 1867, marking the end of cased images. Tintypes were produced in various other forms until about 1930.

Guide to Identifying Ambrotypes and Tintypes

The easiest way to identify either an ambrotype or a tintype is simply to remove the image from its case, if possible, and look at the back of the plate. If it is glass, then it is an ambrotype. If it is black, gray, or brown-coated metal, it is a tintype. However, when removal is not possible, distinguishing an ambrotype from a tintype can be tricky.

The shadows in an ambrotype are usually created through application of a black backing; therefore, they exhibit an almost three–dimensional value when examined closely—as if the shadows and highlights are on separate planes.

The exception to this rule is an ambrotype made on dark glass, which resembles a tintype until removed from the case and examined. Tintypes are the least "dramatic" of cased images, generally exhibiting minimal contrast range and no whites. In tintypes, both highlights and shadows will appear to be on the surface of the plate.

Fig. 2-1. John Christopher Draper, 1/4-plate ambrotype.

A rare and ironic ambrotype occupational portrait of the son of the man purported to be the first American to produce a daguerreotype, John William Draper. All occupational images are prized by collectors and those of historical interest are particularly valuable. (Courtesy of Charles Schwartz, Ltd.)

History of the Ambrotype and the Tintype

During the early years of paper photography, a thin sheet of paper was used as the negative. The lack of transparency and fibrous texture of these negatives led to research for an alternative material. While glass had been suggested for many years, it was not until 1851 that an English sculptor, Frederick Scott Archer, devised the best method for applying a sensitized coating to the plate. Archer suggested the use of collodion, a thick, sticky liquid which had previously been used by military physicians as a sort of liquid bandage. The collodion, when mixed with sensitizing chemicals, clung tightly to the glass and formed a light–sensitive surface. The only drawback was that the sensitivity quickly dwindled as the collodion began to dry. The plate, therefore, had to be exposed as quickly as possible after coating, suggesting the name "wet process."

A number of photographers, including Archer, noticed that when a thin collodion negative was viewed with a black backing using reflected light, the image appeared positive. In July of 1854, Bostonian James Cutting took out three U.S. patents based on this concept. In Cutting's patented process, a thin negative was made by slightly underexposing the plate. Then a second sheet of clear glass was sealed to the image with balsa gum (this seal was supposed to protect the image from dust and scratches, but, as we will see, this process did more harm than good). After a coat of black varnish was applied to the back of the plate or to the back of the case, the finished image was placed under a mat and preserver, and then cased or framed. During the early years, daguerreotype cases were used. Then, as the ambrotype become more popular, cases were made deeper to allow for the double thickness of glass.

The suggestion for the name *ambrotype* came from Cutting's associate Marcus Root, who based the name on the Greek word *ambrotos*, meaning "immortal." Since most existing ambrotypes are of people who passed away more than a century ago, the name now seems very appropriate. In France and England, the process was called "collodion positive," and ambrotypes were advertised as "daguerreotypes on glass," or by various trade names, such as Verrotype (used by Lanes Photographic Gallery, Brighton, England).

By 1856, ambrotypes were being made by almost every major gallery in America and by many in Europe. Cutting and his partner, Isaac Rehn, traveled extensively, selling licenses and promoting the process. Even though the finest examples never compared to the richness of the daguerreotype, ambrotypes were cheaper and easier to make, and, lacking the reflectivity of the daguerreotype, were easier to view.

During the peak years, 1856 and 1857, ambrotype production surpassed daguerreotype production and signaled the beginning of the end for the daguerreotype. At the same time, two other forms of photography were about to make their debut: the carte de visite and the tintype.

The major faults of the ambrotype were fragility and the necessity of using a black backing. Neither of these problems existed in the tintype process.

While experimenting with the ambrotype in 1854, Hamilton Smith, a chemistry professor at Kenyon College in Ohio, tried using blackened sheet iron instead of glass. He found the resulting images to be nearly equal in quality, more durable, and cheaper and easier to make. One of Smith's students, Peter Neff Jr., struck a bargain to bankroll the invention in exchange for patent rights to the process, which they called the "melainotype." The patent was issued Feb. 19, 1856. In the fall of that year, Neff exhibited a number of melainotypes at the Fair of the Amer-

Fig. 2-2. Four Couples, 1/4-plate ambrotype.

The slow sensitivity of ambrotypes made photographing large groups a challenge. Each person had to hold absolutely still for three to five seconds or more. Group ambrotypes are highly sought after by collectors. (Collection of Gregory Fried)

ican Institute, where his work received a bronze medal. The resulting publicity aroused interest, but stringent licensing requirements hampered expansion.

As the tintype business began to grow, a competitive plate manufacturing firm was opened in Lancaster, Ohio, by Victor Griswold, a former Kenyon College student. Griswold called his product "ferrotype plates," a name which, despite early opposition, eventually won out over Neff's "melainotype."

Both Neff and Griswold were manufacturing their plates on a large scale when photography's greatest boon was created by the Civil War. Thousands of young soldiers visited the tintypist before heading into battle, and hundreds of itinerant tintypists headed their wagons for the battlegrounds. For many, the lowly tintype would provide a last cherished look at loved ones (see Chapter 11).

Fig. 2-3, 2-4 Coming and Going, 1/6-plate ambrotypes.

While ambrotypes of a subject's front and back are not unique, they are uncommon and highly prized by collectors. In most cases, such images are produced to show off fashionable clothing and/or hair. This example is particularly endearing as well. (Collection of Richard and Gloria Schroeder)

One of the most historic uses of the tintype took place during the 1860 presidential campaign. Some 300,000 campaign buttons were produced containing a tiny tintype of candidate Abraham Lincoln. The image was taken by Mathew Brady on the day of Lincoln's famous Cooper Union speech. President Lincoln would later state: "Brady and the Cooper Union made me President of the United States."

Lincoln played an important part in the history of photography by being one the few (and most recognized) presidents to be photographed by every major process being used in America during his life span (daguerreotype, ambrotype, tintype, carte de visite, and albumen print).

While the carte de visite was the process of choice for big city galleries, tintypes were made on a large scale throughout the war years. Although production then waned, tintypes continued to be produced as beach and carnival novelties until after the turn of the century.

Even though a tintype process was demonstrated in France three years before the American

patents were issued, it never really caught on in any European country and was always known as "the American process."

The Ambrotype/Tintype Process

At the heart of both the ambrotype and the tintype processes was a substance called collodion. Some operators made their own by dissolving guncotton in alcohol and ether; others purchased their collodion, premixed, from suppliers such as Edward Anthony in New York. Anthony advertised a variety of ambrotype supplies in 1856.

Making an ambrotype was a messy proposition, leaving sticky collodion residue to clean and silver nitrate–stained fingers. First, the glass plate had to be thoroughly cleaned to remove dirt and oils; then the ambrotypist (or an assistant) poured a small amount of collodion onto the center of the glass and tilted the plate in all directions until the sticky liquid spread to the edges. In a darkroom, working by the filtered light of a candle, the coated plate was immersed in a tray of silver nitrate for a few minutes and then quickly removed and placed in a shield. From this point, time was of the essence, for the plate would quickly lose its sensitivity as it began to dry. The shield was taken to the operating room and inserted into the waiting camera.

Fig. 2-5. Effect of Black Backing, 1/6-plate ambrotype.

Nothing more than a weak negative, ambrotypes on clear glass require the addition of a black backing to appear positive. This effect is clearly demonstrated in this illustration, where a half-black, half-white backing is used.

Because the ambrotype, being less sensitive than a daguerreotype, sometimes required more than 30 seconds of exposure, the infamous head-rest was always used for indoor portraits. During pleasant weather, the ambrotypist often set up an outdoor operating room where exposure times could be reduced to as little as 5 seconds.

After exposure, the operator quickly returned the shield to the darkroom, where the still-tacky plate was set into a tray of pyrogallic acid. By candlelight, the image could be judged as correctly developed, then the plate was fixed, washed, and dried. Now the ambrotype was ready for application of color and placement in a case.

Fig. 2-6, 2-7 The Hidden Mom, 1/6-plate ambrotype.

Collectors are occasionally surprised by what lies hidden on that portion of the image covered by the mat. In this case, the subject is a baby, but the mother's hand and near proximity were required to get the shot. In some cases, the mother was placed behind the child and was covered by a drape. (Collection of Gregory Fried)

Fig. 2-8. Scraped backing, 1/6-plate ambrotype.

In a typical ambrotype, the background is necessarily a dingy gray, as seen in the image on the right. The image on the left has had the backing scraped away to produce a brighter, contrasting background. In this particular image, a blue foil was later used as a backing to add color to the photograph. The baby in the image may be sleeping, but it is more likely that this is a postmortem photograph. (Collection of Gregory Fried)

Fig. 2-9. Woman Leaning on Head Brace, 1/6-plate ambrotype.

Only a few images exist in which the head brace is used for other than its intended purpose. This one is even more striking due to the woman's fashionable attire, the hat held in hand, and the overall quality of the image.
(Courtesy of Julie and Dominic Santangelo)

As previously mentioned, a black background was necessary to produce the appearance of a positive ambrotype image. During the early years, this was done by simply blackening the bottom of the case. Then it was noticed that the crispness of the blacks in the image were directly affected by the quality and smoothness of the backing. Ambrotypists experimented with a variety of backings, including metal plates coated with Japan varnish, dark velvet material, painted cardboard, and black varnish on the back of the plate. A number of ambrotypes were made on "coral glass," a dark, violet-colored plate which required no backing. The best results were always achieved by minimizing the space between the surface emulsion (which made up the highlights) and the backing (which produced the shadows). The importance of this can easily be seen in extant ambrotypes with dirty or damaged backings (see Chapter 4).

In rare cases, the ambrotypist might scrape away that portion of the emulsion surrounding the subject and blacken only the area behind the

Fig. 2-10. Horse-drawn Wagon in Snow, half-plate ambrotype.

One of the complaints of the ambrotype process was the difficulty in obtaining true whites. This unusual 1870's snow scene shows that, after the process had ceased to be popular, some photographers continued to work to improve the process. A rare and very collectible ambrotype. (Courtesy of Charles Schwartz, Ltd.)

subject. Then, by the application of a white background, the effect of a photograph on milk glass could be produced.

Because ambrotypes were considerably thicker than daguerreotypes, manufacturers began producing thinner mats and deeper cases to accommodate the change. Since one of the primary attractions of the ambrotype was its low cost, case makers also began cutting back on quality standards to produce appropriately "cheap" cases.

The tintype (melainotype, ferrotype) process was identical to the ambrotype process except that tintypes used a thin iron plate painted with black Japan varnish. This plate was coated with collodion, sensitized, exposed, and developed as previously described for the ambrotype process. The image was then adorned with mat, coverglass, preserver, and case. At the beginning of the Civil War, tintypes were sometimes placed in carte de visite-sized sleeves, which could be easily carried in a soldier's Bible and could be displayed in carte de visite albums at home.

Improvements in the wet-plate process reduced tintype exposures to under 5 seconds, and even less with the newly invented "fast" camera lenses. Multi-lens cameras with revolving backs produced tiny "gem" tintypes, sold cheaply by the dozen. The backs of tintypes in carte de visite sleeves occasionally contain the tintypist's price list. One such advertisement for Ohlwiler's in Erie, Pennsylvania, shows the price for gem tins as 6 for 50 cents or 16 for $1. Tintype prices were lowered even more by simply giving the plate a coat of varnish and handing it to the customer without a case or sleeve.

After 1880, tintype dry plates were purchased presensitized from the manufacturer. The boardwalk tintypist would load all of the plates in the morning, then expose and develop them at his or her leisure.

Fig. 2-11, 2-12 Julia's Poem, 1/9-plate ambrotype.

Collectors who make a flea market or estate sale purchase are always anxious to remove the image from its case and see what treasure may be hidden behind–perhaps the name of the photographer or sitter, a lock of hair, a love note, or even a poem. This one reads: "Oft thine eyes shall fondly trace, These simple lines I shall sketch, What'er the time, What'er the place, Think of me, Oh think of me... Your Friend, Julia." (Collection of Gregory Fried)

Collecting Ambrotypes and Tintypes

The collecting of ambrotypes and tintypes is primarily an offshoot of daguerreotype collecting. Therefore, much of the information provided in the section in Chapter 1, "Collecting the Daguerreotype," applies to this collecting category as well, and will not be repeated here. Because most ambrotypes and tintypes are priced considerably lower than equivalent daguerreotype images, they are an excellent choice for beginning collectors or those on a budget. This is not to say that rare and expensive examples do not exist, as we shall see.

What to look for

As for daguerreotypes, when contemplating an ambrotype or tintype purchase, ask yourself the following three questions:

1. Is the image content unusual? By 1860, photography in its several forms was commonplace; therefore, the pool of ordinary images from this time period is large. As with the daguerreotype, anything which makes a particular ambrotype or tintype image stand out from the rest makes it more collectible.

2. *What is the condition of the piece?* The collector of ambrotypes quickly learns to tell the difference between irreparable damage to the image emulsion and damage to the backing that can be repaired (see Chapter 4). Both ambrotypes and tintypes are subject to cracking of the emulsion and oxidation, which sometimes forms a dark halo around the image. Damage of this type lessens the value of a piece and cannot easily be arrested or repaired.

3. *Is the price right?* Just as the consumer of the late 1850s was fooled by the advertisement for "daguerreotypes on glass," many sellers today still don't know the difference. Just because an ambrotype or tintype is contained in a brass frame and leather case, doesn't make it as valuable as a daguerreotype. Unfortunately, many of the more common images are overpriced as a direct result of this confusion. However, when purchasing better-quality pieces from knowledgeable dealers, this will not ordinarily be a problem.

*Fig. 2-13. Girl in Fancy Hat and Cape,
1/6-plate ambrotype.*

(Collection of Gregory Fried)

Fig. 2-15. Injured Brother, 1/6-plate ambrotype.

*(Collection of Richard and Gloria Schroeder)
Seemingly ordinary images can be quite valuable
when examined in greater detail. The little girl's outfit
(Fig. 2-13) is quite unusual for a basic studio portrait.
The man (Fig. 2-14) has his arm in a sling and holds a
Bible in his hand. In the photo above, the little boy to the
left has a scar on his cheek, but an even more thorough
examination reveals that he is missing a foot as well.*

*Fig. 2-14. Man with Sling and Bible,
1/6-plate ambrotype.*

(Collection of Gregory Fried)

Availability/Value Classifications

The common ambrotype or tintype ($15 to $50)

Of the total number of ambrotype and tintype images available to the collector, approximately 60 percent are considered *common*. As with the daguerreotype, *common* images are ordinary portraits of ordinary people. For the collector of faces, here is a seemingly endless supply: children, families, twins, the elderly, and so on. Those interested in fashion can find anything from working clothes to ball gowns. Plate sizes of 1/9 and 1/6 abound; 1/4 and 1/16 sizes are slightly more valuable. In all categories, ambrotypes are slightly more valuable than similar tintypes.

Examples of recent sales (all cased images):

1/9 plate, ambrotype, simple portrait of young
  woman, antique shop, $20

1/6 plate, tintype, girl in pink-tinted dress,
  antique shop, $27

Fig. 2-16. A Cute Puppy, 1/9-plate ambrotype.

Images of animals are highly prized by collectors, and those in which the animal has not moved and blurred the picture are very uncommon. This super-sharp ambrotype of an adorable puppy is indeed a prize. (Collection of Randy New)

1/6 plate, ambrotype, portrait of man in top hat, antique shop, $35

1/16 plate, tintype, basic portrait of man, antique shop, $38

1/6 plate, tintype, twin girls holding hands, dealer, $45

1/6 plate, tintype, girl standing in front of brick wall, dealer, $45

1/9 plate, ambrotype, close-up of baby in Union case, antique shop, $50

The uncommon ambrotype or tintype ($50 to $200)

About 25 percent of the available base falls into the *uncommon* category, which is comprised largely of American Civil War images (see Chapter 11). Also included here are postmortems, some occupational portraits, and tintype views.

Fig. 2-17. Abolitionist and Wife, 1/6-plate ambrotypes.

Careful attention should be paid to identification of accompanying images and the buyer should make every attempt to determine the provenance of a piece, especially the family name, if known. These images were purchased from an estate sale and identified as abolitionist David James Van Meter and his wife. The book in Van Meter's hand is the History of Slavery and the Slave Trade, by W. Blake. (Collection of Gregory Fried)

Fig. 2-18.

Close-up of book in Fig. 2-17.

Examples of recent sales:

1/16 plate, tintype, basic head shot of man in Union case, antique shop, $65

1/4 plate, tintype, bearded man wearing fraternal ribbon, dealer, $75

1/6 plate, ambrotype, family group of five, dealer, $75

1/6 plate, tintype, basic portrait of attractive woman in Union case, antique shop, $75

1/6 plate, tintype, man in slouch hat smoking pipe, dealer, $100

1/9 plate, ambrotype, occupational–man in apron with knife, dealer, $100

1/4 plate, ambrotype, two ladies with music books in lap, auction, $115

1/4 plate, ambrotype, attractive Spanish woman with comb in hair, dealer, $125

1/6 plate, tintype, two men in sailor clothing, dealer, $125

1/6 plate, tintype, man on horseback, dealer, $125

1/6 plate, ambrotype, well-dressed woman in ornate chair by Hamilton, auction, $135

1/6 plate, tintype, occupational, man with unknown tools, dealer, $160

1/2, tintype, family group of six in Moroccan case, antique shop, $190

The rare ambrotype/tintype ($200 to $1,000)

Less than 15 percent of the available base can be considered *rare*. Most occupational portraits and images containing tools, weapons, musical instruments, or animals are considered *rare* (especially ambrotypes). Ambrotype landscape views and some unusual tintype views are also *rare*. Some post-mortems, images of animals, and history-related images fall into this category as well.

Examples of recent sales:

1/16 plate, tintype, basic head shot of black woman, dealer, $200

1/6 plate, tintype, standard portrait of black woman, dealer, $225

1/6 plate, ambrotype, girl in yellow-tinted dress by Walker, auction, $355

1/4 plate, ambrotype, husband and wife pair in separate cases by Vance, auction, $475

Fig. 2-21. Nicely-dressed Black Woman, 1/4-plate ambrotype.

Most ambrotype portraits of African-Americans were taken just prior to, or during, the Civil War, making them valuable historic documents. This example is of particularly high quality, and the original shows delicate tinting of the chair-back and drapery. (Collection of D. J. Knowles)

half plate, ambrotype, father-daughter seated beside picture of absent mother, auction, $488

1/4 plate, tintype, commercial carriage with eight passengers, dealer, $500

1/4 plate, ambrotype, horse and carriage with driver and passenger, auction, $500

Fig. 2-19. The Fencers, CDV-sized tintype.

1/4 plate, ambrotype, two girls posed with Indian woman, auction, $546

1/6 plate, ambrotype, post-mortem of woman with Bible, auction, $575

1/6 plate, ambrotype, pair of little girl in hat—front and back, auction, $575

1/4 plate, tintype, hand-tinted bare-chested man with gun and dog, auction, $750

1/6 plate, ambrotype, stage coach in front of building, auction, $800

1/4 plate, ambrotype, two black children standing by white baby in buggy, auction, $1,000

Fig. 2-20. Equestriennes, half-plate ambrotype.

Rare images come in a variety of forms. The somewhat humorous tintype of fencers (Fig. 2-19) was one of a set of three that sold at auction in 1998 for $402. The large-plate ambrotype is unique for both the subject and the camera angle. It sold at auction in 1998 for $862. (Courtesy of Swann Galleries, Inc.)

Fig. 2-22. Children in Goat Cart, 1/6-plate ambrotype.

Fig. 2-23. Plains Indian, 1/6-plate tintype.

Outdoor images of people engaged in activities are quite rare. In this case, the combination of children, a goat, a cart, and an outdoor setting make for a highly desirable, collectible photograph. (Collection of Gregory Fried)

Images of Native Americans have risen steadily in value over the past two decades. This loose tintype was one of a pair that sold at auction in 1998 for $1,092 the lot. (Courtesy of Swann Galleries, Inc.)

The premium ambrotype or tintype ($1,000 and up)

Premium ambrotype or tintype images are usually unique views or subjects, large plates, history–related, and/or portraits of notable people.

Examples of recent sales:

1/9 plate, tintype, man and boy in fake mustache with stack of cameras, auction, $1,100

Half plate, ambrotype, theatrical performer in odd costume with sword, auction $1,150

1/9 plate, tintype, copy of portrait of Lincoln before his election, $3,150

1/4 plate, ambrotype, Polynesian couple, auction, $9,775

Half-plate, ambrotype, High Chiefess Konia of Hawaii, auction $9,775

The Future of Ambrotype and Tintype Collecting

As is true for daguerreotypes, ambrotype images are now being recognized as being historically important, and prices are rapidly rising in all categories. By meeting the requirements for collectibility–rarity, aesthetics, and emotional attraction–the ambrotype and cased tintype provide wide-ranging possibilities for the collector and investor.

Fig. 2-25. Bayard Taylor, 1/6-plate tintype.

While his name may not be immediately familiar to those who are not students of early California, Taylor is known as one of the premier chroniclers of the Gold Rush, making this image extremely valuable. Photographs of state and regional importance can be just as valuable as those of nationally recognized people and places. (Collection of Joseph T. Silva)

Fig. 2-26. Indian Family, 1/6-plate tintype.

A rare and endearing portrait of an Indian family in "Americanized" dress, this image is a valuable historical document and a treasured "find" for any collector. Images of Native Americans are constantly rising in value. (Collection of D. J. Knowles)

Fig. 2-24. Konia of Hawaii, half-plate ambrotype.

Early Hawaiian images are quite rare, and images of Hawaiian royalty even more so. This wonderful large-format, cased ambrotype of High Chiefess Konia sold at auction in 1998 for $9,775. (Courtesy of Swann Galleries, Inc.)

Fig. 2-27. Post Office, Vacaville, California, half-plate ambrotype.

Large format cased images of identified buildings, streets, and/or towns are premium collectible images, realizing high prices at sale or auction. Taken in the late 1850s, this image is one of the earliest extant photographs of a U.S. Post Office in the state of California. (Courtesy of Charles Schwartz, Ltd.)

Fig. 2-28. Forbestown, California, half-plate ambrotype.

While ambrotypes are generally found in cases, this rare view of a California town, taken in the late 1850s, is housed in a wonderfully designed wood and tooled leather frame. An image and frame of this type is a rare find, an important historical document, and a premium collectible piece. (Collection of Joseph T. Silva)

Fig. 2-29. Man with Black Boy and Dog, half-plate ambrotype.

Believed to be a slave owner and his son, this large-format ambrotype is a rare document of early America. (Collection of D. J. Knowles)

Fig. 2-30. Female Furrier, 1/6-plate tintype.

Occupational images are those in which the subject wears clothing or is posed with tools that are associated with a particular trade. Occupational images are highly sought after and prized by collectors. (Collection of D. J. Knowles)

Fig. 2-31. Cigar Smokers, 1/6-plate tintype.

A rare and highly collectible image of two black men wearing large hats and smoking cigars. The elaborate props and background indicates that this image may have been made after the waning days of the cased image. (Collection of D. J. Knowles)

Fig. 2-32. Crossed Arms, 1/9-plate tintype.

Occasionally an image will be found that invites conjecture as to its purpose. Is the sitter a professional fighter, or giving a cryptic signal that he is a prisoner? The possibilities are endless. Images of this type are prized by collectors. (Collection of Gregory Fried)

Fig. 2-33. Girl with Kitten.

Images containing animals have increased greatly in value over the past decade. Images of children with animals are particularly valuable. (Collection of Gregory Fried)

Fig. 2-34. Santa Rosa House Hotel, half-plate ambrotype.

(Collection of Joseph T. Silva)

Fig. 2-35. Pages from a Gem Tin album.

With the advent of multi-lens wet-plate cameras came the ability to produce a dozen or more tiny images on a single-plate. These could then be mounted in carte de visite sleeves, or placed in albums designed for the purpose. The pages shown here are from a school album, with the names of the students and teachers written under each tin.
(Collection of the author.)

CHAPTER 3

IMAGE CASES

Cases were produced with a wood-frame base covered in paper, cloth, or leather, and were molded from plastic, made from a mixture of shellac and woody fibers.

Introduced	1839
Union case	1852
Peak years	1853-1864
Waned	late 1860s

History of the Image Case

While the primary concern of this book is the collection and appreciation of photographic images, cases are discussed as well because of the important part they played in the preservation of early images, as well as because of their historical, aesthetic, and monetary value. Even though the cased image is priced as a package, the value of the case itself is often a separate consideration in the value of the piece. This chapter provides information essential to understanding this concept.

Fig. 3-1.

Early cases were made of leather or papier mâché and lightly embossed. Written on the silk pad inside the case is the date the image was taken: Aug. 20, 1846. (Collection of the author)

The use of a leather case to enclose and protect photographic images was adopted in the United States and England almost immediately after the introduction of daguerreotypy in 1839. Similar cases had been previously used to hold both miniature paintings and various products of the jeweler's art. After 1840, the new daguerreian industry required more cases in one year than the

total that manufacturers had produced since cases had first been introduced.

Early cases in both England and the United States were of a wood-frame construction, covered in plain Moroccan leather, but by 1842, American cases were on their way to becoming elaborately embossed works of art. Many of these were designed by the daguerreotypists themselves. Mathew Brady, John Plumbe, and William Shew all produced cases during the early years.

Fig. 3-2.

William Shew was one of the earliest and most prolific of case makers. His label appears in various forms, but does not appear in every case he manufactured. (Courtesy of Paul K. Berg

By 1850, there were a number of successful case manufacturers throughout the eastern United States. It is unfortunate that most of these companies did not imprint their names on their work so that existing designs could be attributed. Because motifs were seldom patented, many popular designs were produced by more than one manufacturer. Cases were purchased, along with other supplies, from distributors like Scovills and Edward Anthony and Co.

Early wood-frame cases are recognizable by their low-relief embossing of simple designs. Both geometric and floral motifs were used beginning in 1845. In 1848, high-pressure stamping machines were introduced that produced deeply pressed patterns with a bold relief. During the 1850s, hundreds of new motifs were designed and manufactured. Geometric and floral patterns were still the most popular, with nature themes (birds, etc.) running a close second. Gilt trim, brightly colored velvet pads (early pads were covered in plain silk), and "superior quality" cases (as indicated by double clasps) were available to the customer at additional cost.

The introduction of the ambrotype and tintype in the late 1850s signaled a drastic change in case making. Cheap cases were required for these "cheap pictures," and price reduction was achieved through a reduction in quality. Those stalwarts who continued to prefer the "high-priced" daguerreotype, or those who just preferred a better case, opted for the plastic Union case.

Various patents were issued for the use of plastic in the production of daguerreotype cases: to Samuel Peck on Oct. 3, 1854; H. Halverson on Aug. 7, 1855; Mark Tomlinson on Aug. 24, 1858; and others. Credit is usually given to Samuel Peck as having been the first to produce and market a perfected thermoplastic case, which he called the "union case." The substance used, primarily a compound of sawdust and shellac (varnish), had been patented (in form) by Nelson Goodyear in 1851 as an improvement in the production of India rubber. The word *union* was used by Peck as a synonym for the word *composition* in his patent, and thereafter became his trade name for this type of case. Since the name was never registered, it was used freely by many other manufacturers.

While the Union case has been (and still is) often referred to as the "gutta-percha" case, it is important to note that no gutta-percha was ever used in the production of photographic cases. This plastic substance, made from the sap of certain Malaysian trees, was used to make items such as small boxes, frames, buttons, and cane heads during the 1850s–but not photo cases. The original patents for various types and styles of Union cases specifically spell out their construc-

tion as "shellac and woody fibers." Those who still use the term gutta-percha in reference to thermoplastic cases are unfortunately misinformed.

Fig. 3-3.

During the early 1850s, a number of case manufacturers were experimenting with plastic. The example pictured here is one of a rare group of transitional cases with a molded plastic motif attached to a wood-frame base. (Courtesy of Paul K. Berg)

Thousands of beautiful designs were conceived and manufactured in plastic from the late 1850s through the Civil War period. A number of improvements to the hinging system of the Union case were implemented as well. By the end of the war, cased images were quickly becoming supplanted by card photographs, and case manufacturers soon began producing new and different plastic products.

Throughout the period of the union case, production of the older style wood-frame case continued as well. Coverings during the late 1850s and early 1860s were usually cardboard or papier mâché, and rarely leather. When demand for cases sharply decreased after the Civil War, case manufacturers turned their efforts to the production of jewelry cases and albums for the then-popular card photographs.

The Manufacture of Image Cases

In the production of the wood-frame case, names were given to the various parts of the housing. The individual pine boards which made up the basic frame were called "rails"; a thin strip of leather which acted as a hinge was called the "outside back" (a smaller piece on the inside was called the "inside back"); the embossed leather, silk, or paper "toppings" were glued to thin sheets of wood called the "cover" and the "bottom"; a velvet pad placed inside the cover was called the "cover pad"; and the small strip of velvet lining the bottom rails (designed to hold the image in place) was called the "pinch pad." These last two items were also called "trimmings." Holding the case shut were either a hook and eye or a spring latch.

In the case factory, young boys and girls were hired to perform the various operations of construction: sawing, gluing, cutting, and pressing. Artists designed the various topping motifs, and engravers transferred the artwork to dies for the press. These designers seldom received credit for their excellent work. Occasionally, one would incorporate his or her name into a tiny corner or edge of the engraving. The names of David Pret-

love, A. C. Paquet, C. Loeke, and the firm of Gaskill and Copper can be found on selected cases. Ideas for motifs came from Greek, Roman, and Egyptian artwork, and from various paintings. Nature, religious, and patriotic themes were also used.

During the peak of case production in the 1850s, a number of particular case styles were created. Cases shaped to resemble tiny books were covered in paper and painted to simulate tortoise-shell, marble, woodgrain, etc. Some of the most beautiful book-style cases were coated with black Japan varnish and inlaid with chips of mother-of-pearl, which were incorporated into paintings of flowers or scenes. A few rare cases were covered entirely with sheets of tortoiseshell, mother-of-pearl, or, more commonly, velvet.

In England, the conservative Britons preferred a plain and elegant case of Moroccan leather. Usually these were stamped with the Royal Seal and occasionally with the photographer's name.

Fig. 3-6.

This early case with the lightly embossed pattern of a boat was one of many leather/papier mâché cases that were designed by David Pretlove. Some versions of the case appear with either the name "E. White" or "Susan" embossed on the banner atop the mast.
(Courtesy of Paul K. Berg)

Fig. 3-5.

The discovery of this rare case label provided a wonderful resource for information about case prices.
(Courtesy of Paul K. Berg)

Fig. 3-7.

Many of the early patents for improvements to the thermo-plastic case were taken out by Samuel Peck. Beginning collectors are cautioned not to apply any significance to the dates found on such labels. These are patent dates that may or may not coincide with the date of the image found in the case. (Courtesy of Paul K. Berg)

Although a few more elaborate cases were purchased from American makers, this plain case would remain in use for daguerreotypes until the end of their production in England in the late 1850s.

Both the English and French also favored the passe-partout style of frame mentioned in Chapter 1. In the production of passe-partout frames, an oval or double-elliptical opening was cut into a sheet of cardboard. The edge of the opening was pressed to give it a curved bias which was usually painted in gilt. The cover-glass was then painted on the inside, allowing only the trimmed opening of the cardboard mat to show. For such a basic process, the effect was quite impressive.

The introduction of plastic Union cases in 1854 provided engravers with a superb new medium for their art. Thermoplastic molds were capable of producing high-relief patterns with sharp lines and extreme detail. Cases could now be formed into oval and octagonal shapes, as well as into the classic rectangle. While plastic cases were subject to chipping, the designs were less likely to wear down than those in leather or other materials and the surface was moisture resistant.

Considerably fewer steps were required in the production of a Union case, and therefore fewer workers were needed. Finely pulverized sawdust

Fig. 3-8.

During the late 1850s, a wave of national pride prompted the manufacture of several patriotic motifs. This trend continued during the Civil War years. Patriotic and war theme cases, such as the "Crossed Cannon" thermoplastic case pictured here, are highly prized by collectors. (Courtesy of Paul K. Berg)

or coal dust was mixed with shellac and color, then run between hot rollers to form a thick paste. Measured quantities of this composition were then subjected to the pressure of steam-heated dies to form the case cover and bottom separately. After cooling, the pieces were removed from the dies and any necessary cutting and polishing was performed. Hinges and clasps were attached, and the inclusion of interior trimmings completed the construction.

One interesting variation of the plastic case came along in the mid-1860s, as case production was declining. Called the "sweetheart" case, it consisted of two interlocking disks. The bottom half was designed to contain a small round tintype, and the top half was a cover which attached by either screw threads or friction. Many of these cases have an uncanny resemblance to a particular brand of cookie, inspiring the modern nickname "Oreo case."

Fig. 3-9.

"Washington Crossing the Delaware," a full-plate thermoplastic case. (Courtesy of Paul K. Berg)

During the Civil War, American manufacturers were turning out both wood-frame and plastic cases in large quantities, many embossed with patriotic themes incorporating flags, shields, eagles, cannons, swords, guns, and Lady Liberty. But as the war ended, so did the demand for image cases. Factories quickly retooled for other products, and the era of the cased image came to an end.

Collecting Wood-Frame and Plastic Cases

Since the time of their production, the beautiful cases that were made to contain and protect images have been admired and collected. Unfortunately, over the years this has been at a great cost to image collectors, as many who collected the case had little respect for the "old photo"

Fig. 3-4.

Large-format cases are among the most valuable. The motif of this half-plate example is called "The Vision of Ezechiel." (Courtesy of Paul K. Berg)

Fig. 3-10.

Fig. 3-11.

All cases with basic geometric designs are not common cases. The case at the top is called the "Eureka Case." It has a leather cover with a metal rim, and is extremely rare and valuable. The case on the bottom is a common papier mâché daguerreotype case of the mid-1850s, with minimal value. (Courtesy of Paul K. Berg)

found inside. Hundreds of images were lost as cases were converted to hold cigarettes, jewelry, hairpins, etc.

In recent years, there has been an increased awareness that in order to preserve the quality of these pieces as historical artifacts, all elements of the cased image must be kept original. Still, the case itself, as an *objet d'art*, has a separately determined value which can add considerably to the overall worth of a particular cased image. As is true for all nineteenth-century works of art, this separate value is based on a number of factors: identification of the artist/manufacturer, quantity produced, condition, and demand. Prices of collectible cases have risen steadily over the past decade, with the largest increase occurring in recent years.

Availability/Value Classifications

Prices listed are for complete cases in good condition, and does not include the value of any image that may be contained therein.

The common case ($15 to $50)

About 75 percent of existing cases are *common* wood-frame cases with simple embossed patterns of a floral or geometric design. Most of these add $15 to $20 to the value of an image, but their primary worth is to protect the image and maintain the originality of the piece. As with images, common cases in the 1/4-, 1/2-, and 1/16-plate sizes are slightly more valuable than cases in other sizes. Early daguerreotype images were contained in plain leather cases, which (when present) can help to confirm an image's age, and therefore add considerably to its value.

The uncommon case ($50 to $250)

The *uncommon* category encompasses approximately 20 percent of the available market. Included are wood-frame cases with unusual coverings (painted, inlaid, etc.) and both the basic and somewhat scarce variations of Union cases.

Almost any plastic case (geometric motif) is worth $50 to $100 when in good condition.

Oval and octagonal cases are prized by collectors, and even common motifs almost always bring $100 to $200. The little round sweetheart cases commonly sell for $80 to $150, when complete and without damage; 1/4 plate-sized Union cases are now *uncommon.*

One-sixth plate Union cases with fruit or flower motifs are worth $75 to $150. Cases which have gilt inlays and impressions, other than trimwork, are *uncommon*, as are those covered in silk or velvet. Wood-frame cases with motifs depicting people and/or animals (not birds) can be quite valuable ($75 to $150).

Fig. 3-12. Fig. 3-13.

Thermoplastic cases in octagonal or oval shapes are particularly sought after by collectors. However, new collectors are cautioned that there is a wide variance in the value of such cases. The shape alone does not determine value.
(Courtesy of Paul K. Berg)

The rare case ($250 to $500)

Examples in the *rare* category make up less than 5 percent of the collectible base. Collectors interested in *rare* cases should obtain the three current authoritative books (see Bibliography) and familiarize themselves with hard-to-find motifs.

Generally, wood-frame cases with unusual coverings or artistic motifs based on paintings, etc., are *rare*. A variety of Union cases with art motifs were produced in limited quantities and are also considered rare, as are most half-plate and full-plate cases.

Fig. 3-14. Fig. 3-15. Fig. 3-16.

Shown are three cases that fit the rare category, typically found only through dealers or auctions. The first (Fig. 3-14) is a double Oreo case made to contain two small round tintypes. The second (Fig. 3-16) is a gold-embossed patriotic case in leather/papier mâché. (Courtesy of Paul K. Berg). The third (Fig. 3-15) is a thermoplastic case with a glass window revealing the image inside.

The premium case
($500 to $2,000)

Very few cases in the *premium* category ever become available. Nearly all are Union cases, and most are half-plate or full-plate size. At the April 6, 1998 Swann Gallery auction, a group of 13 mostly Union cases, including the half-plate case, "The Wedding Reception," sold for $2,530.

Fig. 3-17. Fig. 3-18.

One of the rarest of image cases, the "Eagle over Earth" case brings premium prices at sale or auction. The case on the bottom is made of mother-of-pearl and tortoise shell, and is extremely rare. (Courtesy of Paul K. Berg)

Case Condition and Care

To command top price, a case must be in near-mint condition. Wood-frame cases generally display some degree of wear on the embossed designs and are highly susceptible to tearing of the spine. Union cases are seldom found without tiny chips or cracks; however, obvious faults reduce the value considerably.

Both types of cases should be stored out of the light and away from heat. They can be cleaned and protected with a gently applied coat of beeswax-based polish. It is highly recommended that all Union cases be wrapped in soft cloth or acid-free paper for protection against chipping.

Fig. 3-19. Fig. 3-20. Fig. 3-21.

Round "Sweetheart" cases were produced from thermoplastic during the waning years of Union case production. In modern times, the cases were given the name "Oreo Cases" because of their uncanny resemblance to the popular cookie. Oreo cases are prized by collectors. (Courtesy of Paul K. Berg)

Fig. 3-22.

Book-style cases can be found with a variety of applied designs. The case above is embossed in gold; the case in Fig. 3-23 is painted; and the case in Fig. 3-24 has silver wire inlays. (Courtesy of Paul K. Berg)

Fig. 3-23.

(Courtesy of Paul K. Berg)

Fig. 3-24.

(Courtesy of Paul K. Berg)

Fig. 3-25.

A variety of wall frames were also made of thermoplastic. The example shown is an elaborate American Colonial design. Plastic wall frames are difficult to locate and prized by collectors. (Courtesy of Paul K. Berg)

Fig. 3-26.

*A number of book-style cases can be found with black
Japan varnish finishes inlaid with mother-of-pearl and
trimmed with painted motifs. Once somewhat common,
these cases have steadily increased in value over the past
decade and are now highly sought-after.*
(Collection of the author)

CHAPTER 4

DOCUMENTATION AND RESTORATION OF CASED IMAGES

Because of the numerous elements which make up a cased image, and because of the various factors involved in the production of cased images, careful examination is necessary both before and after purchase. Often this examination can reveal variations which, once known, can add considerably to the value of the piece.

Before the Purchase

The first step in examining a prospective purchase is to determine the type of process that was used to create the image. This may sound simple, but as we shall see, it is not always easy to do. Many sellers have no idea what they are selling. An item may be labeled incorrectly or given a general description such as "old photo." Daguerreotypes should be obvious unless the image is badly tarnished. Even then, some evidence of the silver plate will usually show through. Distinguishing between an ambrotype and a tintype, however, can sometimes be quite difficult.

If the seller will allow removal of the plate packet, the back of the metal or glass plate makes identification simple. However, when removing the image from the case is not allowed, a careful examination under bright light will reveal some "clues." In most ambrotypes, the collodion image is on the top of the plate and the black backing is on the bottom. When viewed at a certain angle, the separation between the highlights of the image on the surface and the shadows beneath is evident. Because they lack this separation, ambrotypes on coral glass are very difficult to recognize without removal from the case.

Adding to the difficulty are those ambrotypes in which the photographer used a blackened metal plate as backing. Viewed from the back, such an ambrotype may appear to be a tintype. An experienced collector can often tell from the weight of the piece that there are two pieces of glass in the packet in addition to the metal plate.

Generally, the overall appearance of a tintype is somewhat lackluster compared to the appearance of an ambrotype. With experience, the collector soon develops the ability to recognize an image type almost on sight.

Examine the image and its case carefully. Brass mats should be examined for name imprints indicating the photographer or gallery. Carefully go over the exterior of the case for tiny imprints of designer names. If possible, remove the image packet and look for imprinted or written information on the back of the plate and in the bottom of the case.

Ambrotypes and tintypes should be examined

Fig. 4-1.

A rear view of this daguerreotype shows that the image package is undisturbed. The original gold-beater's tape seal is in place and the bends in the preserver flaps appear to be original.

for cracked and flaking emulsion, as these ailments are irreversible and detract considerably from the value. Scratches and rub marks on a daguerreotype usually indicate that the image has been removed from its case and the seal, if there was one, is broken. A halo of tarnish is not uncommon on daguerreotype images and can actually add to the character of the piece. However, extensive tarnish, stains, oxides (white film), or salting (green flecks) can detract from the value of an image and will probably worsen with age. Daguerreotype images that show no evidence of tarnish have either been cleaned or they are modern images. Cleaned images are less valuable because of the uncertainties involved in the cleaning process (see "Restoration," presented later in this chapter).

The faking of early images has become more common during the past decade, primarily because of the larger numbers of people now involved in modern daguerreotypy and collodion photography. For the most part, these modern practitioners

Fig. 4-2.

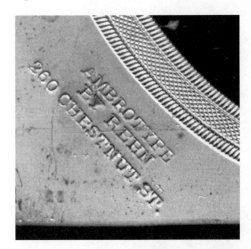

Not all blind stamp impressions are as obvious as this Rehn embossing. It is not unusual for a collector to discover the photographer's name on the mat long after the purchase. All elements of the image package should be thoroughly examined for names and/or initials.

Fig. 4-3.

Elements of a cased image include, from left, the case, the image, the mat, the glass, and the preserver. Additionally, one may find a seal of paper or tape and/or a photographer's advertising card. (Art by David White)

are honest men and women who usually mark their work so that it can not be passed off as original. However, there are those who have, and will go to the considerable effort required to make both the subject and the image appear to be from the 19th century, with the express intention of passing it off as an antique. Also, there are those who will take an honest photographer's work and remove whatever safeguard he or she has used in order to sell the image as an early piece. Keep in mind that modern fakes will usually appear as *rare* or *premium* category images sold at bargain prices by individuals rather than established dealers.

After the Purchase

Nearly every cased image in existence has survived for more than 100 years. Through careless handling, you can destroy one in seconds!

Throughout the examination and documentation process, never allow anything to contact the image surface. Handle the plate with clean hands (white cotton photo gloves are even better), and only by the edges. Stay away from moisture of any kind. Work on a large, flat surface covered with a clean, soft, dry cloth.

Several different methods can be used to remove an image packet from its case. One is to gently tap the case against your cupped hand so that the image packet falls out into your palm. This method requires considerable practice, and still may result in a torn spine. The most common method is to pry the packet carefully out with a thin-bladed table knife, a tiny jeweler's screwdriver, or a dental pick–taking care not to damage the pinch pad. The preferred method, however, is to use a small suction cup attached to the cover glass–provided the glass is not cracked or broken. Regardless of which method is used, also be careful not to damage the case spine (if extant) and, if the packet is not held together by a preserver, be prepared for the possibility that the elements are simply lying loose in the case. If so, the mat could scratch the plate during the removal process.

Documenting the Image

Begin your documentation by writing down a general description of the piece. Include the case design and motif, mat shape, preserver style, and any imprints you may find. If the image is a daguerreotype, make note of whether the plate has been galvanized (silver on back) or gilded (gold tone), and also note whether the seal is intact. If the original sealing tape or paper backing still holds the plate securely to its cover-glass, stop here. Make sure you have written down all perti-

Fig. 4-4. Fig. 4-5.

 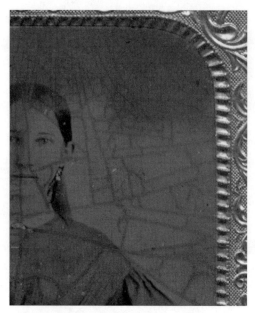

Both tintypes and ambrotypes are subject to crackling of the emulsion. Such damage is irreversible, and further deterioration can only be arrested by a professional conservator.

nent information and return the packet to its case. If no seal is evident or if the existing seal is completely broken, the packet may be separated for further documentation.

It is very important that the preserver be unfolded so that the flaps are at a right angle to the back of the plate. If they are pushed back without unfolding, the preserver will very likely break at the corners. Once the preserver is folded back, the plate can be lifted straight up and away from the mat, taking care not to scrape or touch the image surface. The previously mentioned suction cup may come in handy here as well.

Examine the front of the plate near the edges for a plate mark. Also make note of any bends, indicating the use of a plate holder (flat, heavy daguerreotype plates date from the early years of the process).

Earliest tintype plates are embossed with either of the two rival plate makers' names and a patent date:
MELAINOTYPE PLATE FOR NEFF'S PROCESS Pat19Feb56
or
GRISWOLD'S PATENTED OCT.26,1856.

Fig. 4-6.

Many wonderful daguerreotypes have been ruined or destroyed by improper handling. This image suffers from a combinations of "rubs" (probably from an attempted cleaning) and scratches from allowing the mat to move across the plate.

Fig. 4-7.

While all images would be more valuable in near-perfect condition, unique examples, like the tintype pictured here, are desirable despite damage or deterioration. (Courtesy of Tom Flood)

Also make note of whether the tintype has been given a coat of varnish. Most tintypes destined for placement in a case were not varnished.

When examining ambrotypes, make note of the type of glass used and the method of viewing (from above or through the plate). If the ambrotype plate appears to be stuck to either the cover-glass or the backing, *do not pull it loose*! To do so may damage the emulsion and destroy the image.

Restoration

Before reassembling the image packet, rinse the mat with denatured alcohol and carefully wipe it with a soft cloth. Then, to achieve maximum archival protection, replace the old cover-glass with modern glass and seal the plate and mat to it with acid-free archival type. The chemicals contained in early glass are the primary source of image deterioration and while cleaning it will make the image look better, it will not stop the corrosive effects that glass produces. It is left up to the individual collector to decide which is more important—leaving original seals intact, or breaking the seal so that the cover glass can be replaced and the image packet archivally sealed.

If you are unable or unwilling to replace the cover glass, wash the old glass with non-detergent soap and hot water; then rinse well, first with hot water, then with alcohol. Make sure both pieces are thoroughly dry before returning them to the packet. After the glass has been cleaned or replaced, the packet can be reassembled and the preserver flaps carefully refolded.

Use a pencil to write pertinent information on the new tape seal, such as the date of resealing, the plate maker (if known), and whether or not the glass was replaced or simply cleaned.

You will be amazed at the difference a new cover glass can make in the appearance of a cased image. For the most part, this should be the only restoration performed by nonprofessionals.

Tintype and ambrotype images cannot be cleaned. Excessive surface dust can be removed with a gentle blast of canned air, but even this procedure can tear away loose emulsion and the chemicals contained in such products may be detrimental to image stability.

Many years ago, conservationists were using a chemical method involving a solution of thiourea to remove excessive tarnish from daguerreotypes. We now know that they were doing permanent harm to the physical structure of the daguerreotype itself. Therefore, *the cleaning of daguerreotypes by any known method is not recommended*. Excessively tarnished daguerreotypes which are proven to be of historical value should be referred to the experts at the Library of

Congress, Smithsonian Institution, or George Eastman House for recommendations.

On common images that are completely obscured by tarnish, the collector may wish to try electrolytic cleaning as described in *The Daguerreotype, Nineteenth-Century Technology and Modern Science* by Susan Barger and William White. (See "Book Dealers" in Appendix C.) This is a very specific process that should only be attempted by those confident in their patience and attentiveness to detail. While the author does not recommend any type of cleaning, he is aware that many new collectors will not be able to resist trying to clean a highly tarnished daguerreotype. Therefore, the specifics of electrolytic cleaning are given at the end of this book, in Appendix D.

Some photo dealers "renew" all common daguerreotypes as a matter of practice, believing that images on clean, shiny silver plates are more attractive to the buyer. In most cases, the plates are cleaned with common commercial silver dip. Daguerreotypes cleaned in this manner are subject to rapid and intense retarnishing, making

Fig. 4-8. Fig. 4-9.

Many new collectors are surprised at the dramatic improvement in apparent image quality afforded by a simple cleaning or replacement of the cover glass on cased images. It is now known that old cover glass is the primary cause of image deterioration, and many collectors replace the glass immediately as a primary conservation step. The image looks better and is better protected.

additional renewal necessary. Such continuous chemical baths will eventually destroy an image. Even one chemical bath does irreparable damage to the physical structure of the daguerreotype by etching its surface and leaving behind destructive films. Electro-ammonia baths are less destructive, but may still leave a residue that can have long-term detrimental effects. Collectors should avoid "renewed" examples and discourage the use of chemical cleaners on daguerreotypes.

Ambrotypes often appear to be badly damaged when the black backing is dirty or flaking. This backing can be replaced with a piece of totally exposed, gloss finish, modern black-and-white photographic paper. This replacement will provide rich blacks in the image, and the paper is acid-free. If you decide to scrape away the old black varnish from an ambrotype plate, first make sure that the image is on the opposite side of the plate, and not under the varnish. Then use extreme care not to damage the image side during the process.

Case repair

A broken case spine can be replaced with a strip of appropriately colored construction paper, carefully glued in place. Given a coat of wax-type shoe polish and "thumbnail" lines, the new spine looks much like the original, and it protects the case and the image from further damage.

Before you hand a cased image to anyone, even a supposed veteran collector, courteously remind them to support both the front and back of the case, and especially the spine.

While it may be tempting to "beautify" an image by trading mats or cases, remember that it is important to keep all elements of a cased image original. Case, plate, mat, and preserver all play an important role in authenticating and dating an image.

Dating the cased image

Of all the factors used in dating an image, the case itself is the least accurate. While specific designs can be traced to certain years, many people, from the original owners to present-day dealers, may have attempted to improve the look and salability of an image by putting it in a

better case. The case may be used, however, to *substantiate* a date arrived at by more reliable means. The image and the plate on which it rests are the best sources for dating information.

Fig. 4-10.

One of the three case spines shown here is a replacement made of "polished" construction paper. (Hint: It's not the one you think it is.) Such a repair, if adeptly performed, does not detract from the value of a piece, and is invaluable in preventing further damage.

While not everyone was a slave to fashion in the nineteenth century, it is a fact that clothing styles changed from year to year, and sooner or later everyone had to buy new clothes. Consequently, sitters' styles of clothing, along with hair styles and beards (or lack thereof), are the best source for estimating the dates of images. Unfortunately, the accuracy of this dating method depends greatly on a thorough knowledge of nineteenth-century fashion. The books recommended in the Bibliography should be very helpful in this area.

Hallmarks

Approximately 60 percent of existing daguerreotype plates are stamped with a hall-mark. The others are "self-cut" plates, trimmed from larger plates by the operator. By studying hallmarks on daguerreotypes with documented dates, and by researching the history of plate manufacturers, historians have developed approximate dates of use for many of these symbols (see Appendix B). This provides the collector with a means of determining a "not-before" production date. For example, an image on a plate containing a Scovills "Extra" hallmark could not have been taken before 1850, which was the first year that hallmark was used.

Also used as an aid in dating are the "config-urations," that is, the marks left on the plate by various tools and devices used in the process. Plate holders requiring bends were not in general use before 1849. However, beveling of plate edges was common as early as 1845. Plier marks are a less reliable source, since other devices were also used to hold the plate; however, heavy plates without plier marks may date from the early years of daguerreotypy (1839 to 1843).

Ambrotype plates bear no dating marks; however, the Cutting Patent method, requiring that a second plate of glass be sealed to the image, was generally discontinued after 1857. Also, the use of coral glass began about the same time. Early tintype plates are thick and heavy, and usually bear the imprint of the manufac-turer. Chocolate-colored tintype plates were produced after 1870, and tiny gem plates were not made in quantity before 1863.

Mat shapes and textures

The decorative mats which were placed between the plate and the glass were usually made of brass, although paper, cardboard, gold foil, and other materials were occasionally used. If the original seal is still intact, or if the shape of the tarnish/oxide pattern matches the shape of the mat, it can be assumed to be original. Because the textures and shapes changed over the years, original mats are a good source for deter-mining an approximate image date without extensive research.

Fig. 4-13.

Preservers were not in general use before 1847. Early versions were stiff and heavy and liable to break at the corners. After 1850, the metal of the preservers was more pliable and the color more "brassy" (less golden) than in first examples. Until the late 1850s, preservers were straight, narrow frames, embossed with simple patterns—rope, stars, daisies, etc. (top). With the introduction of ornate mats, a fancy lightweight preserver was also made available (center). Finally, an even lighter version was designed with inward "points" at the corners and centers of the sides (bottom).

Fig. 4-11.

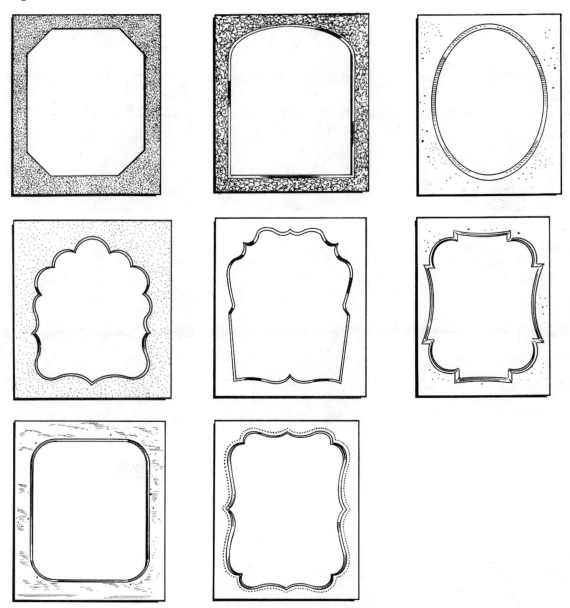

The first two mat shapes in the top row were very popular throughout the 1840s but were seldom used after 1850. Early versions have a pebble finish; later examples are "sandy." A few matte-finish examples were produced during the early 1850s, but these are uncommon.

Oval mats (top row, right) were produced throughout the era of the cased image, while acorn-shaped mats (second row, left) with a sandy finish were produced in limited quantities during the mid-to-late 1840s. Oval mats can be found in a variety of finishes and with various stamped or embossed ornamentations.

The two other unusual mat shapes in the center row (center and right) were produced during the late 1840s and in use until about 1851. Early examples have a sandy finish; later examples are matte.

Production of the two shapes in the bottom row began in the mid-1840s. A sandy or matte finish was used until 1850, after which these mats were produced exclusively in matte, often with stamped or engraved ornamentation. These were the two most popular shapes from the mid-1850s and were embossed with ornate designs from the late 1850s on. One variation of the double-elliptic mat dating from the early 1850s was quite heavy and stamped with a crosshatch design near the opening.

Fig. 4-12.

As daguerreotype became more popular and other forms of photography were introduced, the manufacturers of brass mats became concerned with producing more attractive pieces. A variety of new shapes were introduced, and the surface of the metal itself underwent several transformations. These design changes play an important part in dating an image.

Early brass mats were comparatively thick and heavy, with a rough pebble texture (top row, left). By the late 1840s, mats were somewhat thinner, with more of a sandy finish (top row, center). Around 1850, the sandy finish gave way to a matte finish (top row, right), and occasionally a fancy decorative pattern was stamped into the surface (second row, left).

With the introduction of the ambrotype in the mid-1850s, mats were made necessarily thinner and almost always embossed with ornate patterns. The mat design shown in the second row, center, dates from the late 1850s and the one in second row, right, dates from the 1860s. On the bottom row, two specialty mats used throughout the 1850s are shown. The first is a super thin gold foil mat attached to a cardboard backing. The second is the thickest and heaviest of brass mats.

Fig. 4-14.

It is the combination of all the elements of a cased image which provides a collector with the information needed to determine an approximate date of production. While no single item can be considered totally accurate, if all of the elements point to the same date, you can be reasonably certain of your dating conclusion. In the above example, the image is an ambrotype on coral glass–first produced around 1856. The mat is a heavy, ornate mat of an unusual style, but the decorations are produced by stamping rather than acid etching, indicating a late 1850's production date. The preserver is a lightweight style with inward points at the corners. This preserver style was introduced around 1858. The case has a narrow spine–the type produced in the mid-1850s for daguerreotypes. Assuming that all elements are original, since everything dates from 1856-58, we can estimate a likely production date of circa 1858.

Photographing Your Collection

The cased image, regardless of its monetary value, is a historical artifact and should be documented for posterity. Because cased images are one of a kind, they cannot be replaced. For this reason, it is highly recommended that you make a photographic copy of each image in your collection. This is best accomplished during your initial examination, while the image is separate from its case. The plate should be photographed without the cover-glass and mat whenever possible.

Any good-quality 35-mm camera with interchangeable lenses is sufficient for documentation. Larger formats may produce images of higher quality, but such cameras are comparatively bulky, hard to focus, and slow to use. Automatic-exposure cameras work well, but they should be equipped with an exposure compensation system which allows for bracketing. You should take an initial reading from a gray card, then bracket your exposures one stop over and under.

Photographing daguerreotypes, like viewing them, requires some adjustment of angle and reflection. A "shield" must be constructed which surrounds the lens and hides all reflections from above the image. A 12" x 12" sheet of cardboard covered with black velvet is perfect for the job. Cut a hole in the center so that it fits snugly around the lens and use a copy stand or tripod to steady the camera. Daguerreotypes also require strong lighting for proper reproduction. A polarizing filter is also helpful. Regardless of the light source, work quickly and do not allow the plate to become heated. Return the image to the protection of its case as soon as possible.

PART II

PHOTOGRAPHY ON PAPER

1 8 3 9 - 1 9 0 0

CHAPTER 5

CALOTYPES

'cal o type: A positive photographic image produced on salted paper from a negative produced in the same manner. Sensitizing agent: silver nitrate; developing agent: pyrogallic acid. Invented by W. H. Fox Talbot (Britain)

Introduced	1841
Peak years	1852-1857
Waned	1859-1862

Guide to Identification of the Calotype and Salt Print

Because calotypes were printed from paper negatives, the image will, to varying degrees, exhibit the fibrous texture of the paper. Salt prints, being made from glass negatives, do not show this texture. In both cases, however, the image will appear to be "embedded" in the paper, as opposed to albumen prints, in which the image appears to sit on the surface of the paper.

History of the Calotype

When news of the daguerreotype first reached England in January of 1839, it came as quite a shock to a British scientist named William Henry Fox Talbot. Since the fall of 1833, Talbot had been experimenting with a process using the camera obscura and chemically treated paper, hoping to "cause these natural images to imprint themselves durably, and remain fixed upon the paper."

His early experimental images, called "photogenic drawings," were actually simple contact negatives made by placing a thin object (lace, leaves, etc.) on the surface of sensitized paper and exposing it to sunlight. By 1835, he had taken pictures of his home using a tiny "mousetrap" camera and had succeeded in fixing the images with a sodium chloride bath. Shortly thereafter, Talbot put aside his experiments for other scientific research and writings, unaware that in France, Daguerre was only four short years from announcing his discovery.

Although the two processes were decidedly different, Talbot, upon hearing of Daguerre's announcement, rushed to London's Royal Institute with samples of his work, determined to claim anteriority over Daguerre's invention. While Talbot's early achievements could not be denied, the resulting images "paled in comparison" to those of Daguerre, an aspersion which angered Talbot and spurred him to search for improvements to the process.

In September of 1840, Talbot discovered an important principle of photography that had been paramount in Daguerre's invention: hidden on the exposed negative was an unseen image. In the calotype process, this latent image could be brought out by development in a gallo-nitrate solution. This discovery shortened exposure times considerably, since previously the sensitized paper had been exposed until it darkened and the image became visible. By this time, Talbot had also discovered that a "re-reversed" or positive image could be made simply by contact-printing the negative onto a second sheet of sensitized paper.

Both Talbot and Daguerre profited from the efforts of Sir John Herschel, who discovered the arresting action of hyposulfate of soda ("hypo").

Fig. 5-1.

Talbot used a number of these tiny cameras, affectionately called "mousetraps," to produce tabotypes of his home several years before he and Daguerre announced their respective processes. (Art by David White)

This hypo fixing bath is still used in modern processes and was an important factor in assuring the permanence of early images. Herschel also coined the term *photograph* and suggested the use of the words *positive* and *negative*.

By 1841, sufficient improvements had been achieved to make Talbot's process commercially appealing and prompt him to secure a patent on Feb. 8 of that year. Unfortunately, the heavy restrictions imposed by this patent, along with continuing unfavorable comparisons to the daguerreotype, severely hampered the spread of calotypy. Similar restrictions imposed by an American patent, granted in 1847, destroyed any chance of the process becoming competitive with the daguerreotype in the United States.

Because of its lengthy exposure times and grainy image, in early years the calotype process was used primarily for outdoor views. Talbot himself traveled extensively throughout Europe, taking calotypes of architectural and scenic views to promote the sale of calotype licenses. While never widely accepted for portraiture, the process was not without its advocates. The first calotype portrait studio was opened on Somerset Street in London by Henry Collen in August of 1841. Because exposure times ranged from a few seconds in the summer sun to as long as 60 seconds in the winter, extensive hand-retouching was employed to provide clients with the best possible likeness. Collen, a former painter, produced excellent "improved" calotype portraits.

In 1844, French daguerreotypist Antoine Claudet struck a bargain with Talbot which would allow him to provide clients at his London studio with a choice of either daguerreotype or calotype portraits. In Scotland, the team of David Hill and Robert Adamson produced some of the most memorable portraits taken by this process.

Fig. 5-2. Choragic Trophy of Lysicrates by Rev. George Bridges, calotype, circa 1850.

Ancient ruins were the preferred subject of early calotype photographers. Early calotypes in good condition by identified photographers bring premium prices at sale or auction. The dealer price for this image: $8,500. (Courtesy of Charles Isaacs)

Fig. 5-3. Forest Landscape by Frank Chauvassaignes, calotype, circa 1857.

This wonderful image of a shadowy glen is a waxed paper print produced from a waxed paper negative. Waxing helped to reduce the fibrous texture visible in prints from plain paper negatives. (Courtesy of Charles Isaacs)

Fig. 5-4. View of Tullichewan Castle, Glasgow, Scotland by Lord Campbell, salt print, ca. 1857.

This salt print was produced from a glass negative, resulting in improved sharpness and finer grain when compared with earlier paper negative calotypes. (Courtesy of Charles Isaacs)

From classic portraits of staunch professors and clergymen to superb studies of common village characters, the callotypes of Hill and Adamson are to Great Britain what the daguerreotypes of Southworth and Hawes are to America.

Today, many calotypes are found in travelogue-type albums or tipped in to printed pages of books. Talbot himself oversaw the production of thousands of images to illustrate his six-part volume titled *The Pencil of Nature* (1844 to 1846). Later, his printers would produce some 6,000 to 7,000 images for insertion in the *Art Union*, a periodical. It is probably due to the lack of quality control during these large-scale projects that many of these calotypes are now extremely faded.

The problem of calotype fading was obvious from the very beginning. Great care was required in the washing stage of the process to achieve any degree of permanence. While Talbot seems to have been quite lax in this area, Hill and Adamson, as well as many French calotypists, took great pains to assure image stability.

In 1844, Louis-Désiré Blanquart-Evrard presented to the French Académie a modified calotype process which used chemically impregnated paper. This process produced superior tone and detail in the image, while providing improved permanence as well. Also, because this process required shorter exposures, Blanquart-Evrard was able to produce large quantities of calotype prints for both display and publication.

The greatest advance in calotypy came in 1851 through the efforts of another Frenchman, Gustave Le Gray. Le Gray's method of waxing the negative resulted in improved transparency, shortened print times, and increased image detail. Moreover, sensitized paper could be prepared several weeks in advance and did not require immediate development. For travel photographers, Le Gray's process was a godsend. For the calotype, this improvement, along with Talbot's relaxation of patent enforcement, marked the beginning of the formative years (1852 to 1857). Both amateurs and professionals began using the process extensively for architectural and travel documentation. In England, a Royal Photographic Society was created with such prominent names as Charles Eastlake, Roger Fenton, and Charles Wheatstone on its roster. Several new calotype cameras were devised, some even with roll magazines.

It was also during this period that a number of paper prints were made from the new collodion or albumenized glass negatives. Because these images are not true calotypes, they are now called "salt prints" to differentiate them from images produced via paper negatives.

While the calotype was enjoying more than moderate success throughout Europe, attempts to stir American interest failed. The Langenheim brothers of Philadelphia purchased the U.S. rights from Talbot in 1849 and attempted to solicit licensees. However, by this time the license-free daguerreotype process was already firmly implanted in the American enterprise system. Daguerreotypists saw no reason to buy a license for a slower process that produced fuzzy images.

In fact, America's foremost calotypist was a Frenchman, Victor Provost. Provost's early images of New York City landmarks are an important historical record of that great city. His high-quality paper negatives have survived to this day in excellent condition.

In Philadelphia, the Langenheims quickly turned their efforts to other areas, introducing a glass negative process in 1849 and popularizing the stereograph beginning in 1850. In 1851, the Langenheims were forced to file bankruptcy because of back payments still owed to Talbot. It was here that the calotype's short, unprofitable visit to America ended.

The discovery of the collodion wet-plate process in 1851 marked the beginning of the end for both the daguerreotype and the calotype worldwide. Although in 1851, their most important years were yet to come; by the 1860s, both processes were virtually obsolete.

The Calotype Process

The specifics of the calotype process changed considerably from its inception in 1833 to the improved process of the 1850s. To make his "photogenic drawings," Talbot used common writing paper, bathed in salt water, followed by a strong solution of silver nitrate. He then placed

Fig. 5-5. Palais de Karnak by Maxime DuCamp, calotype, ca. 1852.

DuCamp was among the premier calotype photographers. This image was produced from a waxed negative. (Courtesy of Charles Isaacs)

an object directly in contact with the paper and exposed the object and paper to sunlight. The areas of the paper not covered would darken, leaving the impression of the object in white. This negative image, called a "reversed copy" by Talbot, was then fixed, either with an additional bath of salt water or a solution of potassium iodide. Many of the images fixed by this method faded away within a few years.

In 1839, Talbot learned of Sir John Herschel's hypo solution, which dissolved silver salts and would "arrest the further action of light." By 1840, Talbot was producing the *talbotype*, a positive image created by placing a reversed copy (negative) in contact with a second sheet of sensitized paper and exposing them to sunlight.

The positive print that was created was called a "re-reversed copy."

With Talbot's discovery of the latent image in 1841, his process changed considerably and the first true calotype was produced. Rather than waiting for the paper to darken and the image to become visible, an exposure was made by uncapping the lens for a predetermined length of time and then bringing the invisible image out (developing it) in a solution of pyrogallic acid. This negative was fixed and contact printed as before, but using the new exposure/development method. Both exposure and printing times were considerably shortened by this method, making the calotype a viable photographic process.

Fig. 5-6. Portrait of a Young Woman by Jones & Brother, salt print, ca. 1860.

The introduction of collodion glass negatives and improvements in sensitivity made the salt print a viable process for portraiture. Quality salt print portraits of this type typically sell for around $500. (Courtesy of Charles Isaacs)

Fig. 5-7. Temple of Dendur, Nubie, by Maxime Du Camp, calotype, 1850s.

Du Camp and other French artists produced some views in quantity for exhibition and sale. This example is marked on the back with the title, plate number, and publisher's credits. (Courtesy of Swann Galleries, Inc.)

The two primary complaints still voiced were the graininess of the image and the lengthy printing times. Both of these problems were somewhat alleviated by the introduction of "waxed negatives" in 1851 by Gustave Le Gray. With Le Gray's method, after the paper was soaked in melted wax and pressed flat, it was sensitized in successive baths of potassium iodide and silver nitrate. Following exposure and development, the nearly transparent waxed paper negative could be printed in considerably less time and the resulting prints were nearly free of the annoying graininess inherent in earlier calotypes.

Most high-quality calotypes still in existence were produced after the improvements of 1851.

Waxed paper negatives have also survived in reasonably good condition and are often used to produce modern prints.

Salt prints

After the introduction of albumen and collodion plates, a large number of glass negatives were printed on "salted paper" in the style of the calotype. These images are generally much sharper, lacking the fibrous texture always evident, to some degree, in prints produced from paper negatives. As noted in the section on collecting calotypes, these "salt prints" date from about the same period as calotypes (approximately 1850 to 1860) and are equally as valuable. There has always been some confusion over these two image types, and the names are often used interchangeably.

Even more confusing are "albumenized salt prints," which have a glossy surface and may be mistaken for standard albumen prints. Careful examination will show that the image of a salt print appears to be embedded in the paper, while an albumen image lies on the surface.

Collecting the Calotype

While salt prints are technically a separate type of image and are usually given separate treatment by auction houses, information pertaining to the collecting of salt prints is identical to that of the calotype as listed here.

Fig. 5-8. Pyramid at Cheops, maker unknown, calotype, circa 1855.

This example sold at auction in 1998 for $2,070. (Courtesy of Swann Galleries, Inc.)

Fig. 5-9. Portrait of William Walker by Webster Brothers, salt print, before 1857.

(Courtesy of Charles Isaacs)

Nearly all calotypes that have survived in good condition are *rare* or *premium* photographs. Even faded and damaged examples are not at all common. There is always the possibility of discovering a previously unknown work at a flea market or estate sale (European collectors have a much better chance of this); however, availability is almost always limited to photographic auctions and dealer sales. Serious collectors should subscribe to the various catalogs offered by those who deal in rare photographs. (See "Collector Resources" appendix.) Less than a half dozen calotypes/salt prints were offered for sale at Swann Galleries' two 1998 auctions.

Calotypes are seldom made available for less than $300, and those offered at this end of the price scale are often unattributed and/or inferior quality examples. You can expect to pay $500 to $1,000 for good, investment-quality pieces and upward of $5,000 for a *premium* specimen. Although this talk of high price and low availability may sound discouraging, there is no better time than now to invest in calotypes. Prices have increased steadily over the past two decades and are expected to continue to rise as more calotypes make their way into permanent collections.

The collector should be aware that calotype fakes are common. As for all rare photographs, buyers should deal only with reputable sources and, when possible, demand the provenance of an image (that is, where did it originate and who were its previous owners?). Collectors should also be wary of "intensified" images. While professional opinions differ, it is the general consensus that all photographs should be left in their natural state (except for basic cleaning). Therefore, prospective buyers should beware of richly toned calotypes that are offered for below market value.

Calotypes are the most delicate of paper photographs and should not be openly displayed. They should be kept in acid-free archival sleeves and/or boxes, in complete darkness, and, under optimum conditions, in a constantly maintained atmosphere of 60 F and 40% relative humidity. As with all photographic images, light, heat, moisture, and careless handling are the calotype's primary enemies.

CHAPTER 6

THE WET PLATE
AND ALBUMEN PRINTS

al 'bu men print: A positive print produced from a glass negative on paper coated with egg whites. Sensitizing agent: silver nitrate; developing agent: pyrogallic acid. Wetplate negative invented by Frederick Scott Archer (Britain). Albumen print invented by L.-D. Blanquart-Evrard (France).

Introduced	1850
Peak years	1860-1890
Waned	1890-1910

Guide to Identifying the Albumen Print

Albumen prints can be found with a variety of outward visual aspects. The shadow tones range from golden brown to reddish to gray-black, and surface textures vary from dull to glossy. Most exhibit yellowing of the albumen base, but this is not always the case. Fortunately, other processes of the same period are distinctively different from the albumen print. Calotypes and salt prints appear to have the image "embedded" in the paper, while the albumen print image lies on the surface. Later processes (gelatin, carbon, platinum) generally exhibit richer tonal quality, often showing some "silvering"–shiny silver coating near the edges–and they lack the yellowish tone of albumen.

History of the Wet Plate and Albumen Prints

The wet-plate process actually forms the foundation for a number of image types discussed in this book. The ambrotype, tintype, carte de visite, cabinet card, and nearly all paper prints produced from 1860 until 1880 made use of the collodion wet-plate process. Of these, only the tintype did not employ the use of a glass plate.

Glass was the logical choice as a base on which to produce negatives, and experiments to that effect were performed as early as 1839 by Sir John Herschel. His method of simply allowing the silver salts to settle on the plate, however, proved to be both inconsistent and impractical. Another type of glass negative was developed by Claude F. A. Niépce de Saint Victor (nephew of

Fig. 6-1. Oregon City 1867 by Carleton Watkins, albumen print.

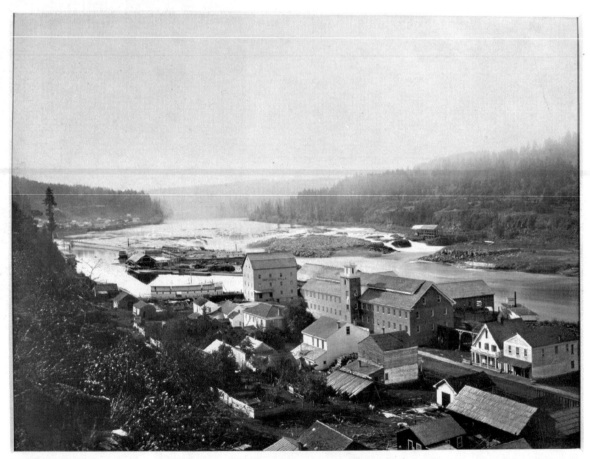

Images depicting early America's Far West are probably the most popular of collectible albumen prints. Carleton Watkins specialized in California, Oregon, and Washington landscapes. (Courtesy of Etherton Gallery)

Daguerre's partner) using albumen (egg whites) as the fixative. This process achieved moderate acceptance and was used in the production of many salt prints prior to the announcement of Archer's collodion process in 1851.

Frederick Scott Archer was an English sculptor who had learned the calotype process in 1847 and had experimented with collodion-coated paper negatives in 1848. The failure of these trials did not discourage his experimentation, and in 1851 he announced the details of a collodion-on-glass process.

Collodion, a mixture of gun cotton, alcohol, and ether, was invented in 1847 by Messieurs Minard and Domote of France. Poured over a surface and allowed to dry, the viscous liquid formed a tough, transparent film and the substance was quickly seized upon by the medical profession as a sort of liquid bandage.

In Archer's process, collodion was poured onto a glass plate and then sensitized, exposed, and developed before the coating could dry. Because of their extreme transparency, collodion negatives were much quicker to print than paper negatives, while also providing better detail and tonal quality.

During the early years of the process (1851 to 1855), most collodion negatives were printed on salted paper, just as Talbot's paper negatives had been, but with an astonishing improvement in quality. These "salt prints" comprise the bulk of paper prints made in France and the United States during this time period (also see Chapter 5). In England, the calotype shared its continuing popularity with the new wet-plate process until the advent of the carte de visite and stereograph after 1856.

As if by providence, at the same time that Archer was perfecting the collodion negative, French calotypist Louis-Désiré Blanquart-Evrard was working on a new printing paper which would soon become an integral and inseparable companion to the wet-plate process. Described before the French Academy of Sciences on May 27, 1850, the process used paper coated with a combination of egg whites mixed with ammonium chloride. This "albumen paper" could be dried and stored for later sensitizing in a silver nitrate bath. The wet plate-albumen print process produced crisp images with superb tonal qualities. Moreover, numerous prints of consistent quality could be produced from one original negative. In 1855, James Waterhouse introduced a method of toning albumen prints with gold chloride which improved image quality even more.

Use of albumen paper skyrocketed during the late 1850s. Factories began to produce precoated paper which photographers could purchase in reams and then cut to size and sensitize as needed. A large number of these manufacturers were located in Dresden, Germany, a town that would become known worldwide as the center of albumen paper production.

Fig. 6-2. Young Girl with Lute by Julia Margaret Cameron, albumen print.

Cameron used soft focus and special lighting to achieve an artistic quality. This small image (4-3/4" x 4") was one of a pair of signed Cameron prints that sold at auction in 1998 for $1,840 the lot. (Courtesy of Swann Galleries, Inc.)

Fig. 6-3. Nude Art Study, albumen print.

Until the latter part of the 19th century, photographs of female nudes were kept well hidden in America while European countries were more accepting of their use as "art studies." This print was one of a group of 39 images of female nudes that sold at auction in 1998 for $3,450, the lot. (Courtesy of Swann Galleries, Inc.)

As the 1860s approached, itinerant and travel photographers found the wet plate-albumen print process well suited for photography on the trail. Throughout Europe, expeditions were sent out to bring back images of the great architectural and scenic views to be found in the Middle East, the Orient, and other "far-off lands." These images would be mass-produced in giant "picture factories" for publication or for sale to the general public.

The factory of Francis Frith, in Reigate, England, maintained a stock of more than 1 million albumen prints. Frith himself undertook an arduous yet productive expedition to Egypt, the Sinai, and Jerusalem, which resulted in the production of a magnificent book, completely illustrated with original 15" x 20" albumen prints. Images from this undertaking were also produced for smaller books, and as stereographs.

With the outbreak of the Civil War, America's photographers turned their lenses toward a grim new subject: death and destruction. On the battlefield, the wet-plate photographer was put to the test of producing quality images of an important historical event, under extremely difficult conditions, and in great danger of personal injury. The most famous of these photo historians was Mathew Brady. Almost killed at the battle of Bull Run, he survived to establish Brady's Photographic Corps, which consisted primarily of himself, Alexander Gardner, Timothy O'Sullivan, and George N. Barnard. In 1863, a riff caused by Brady's unwillingness to give specific photographic credit to his associates resulted in the disbanding of the group; however, all four continued to document the war until its conclusion.

After the war, O'Sullivan, Gardner, and Barnard set off with heavily laden packmules to document Westward expansion. Spectacular views of vast, unspoiled lands and the Native Peoples who resided there were brought back from the several expeditions taken well into the 1870s. Also prominent among Western photographers was William Henry Jackson, who left his studio in Omaha, Nebraska, to document the route of the transcontinental railway. Photographing the back trails of California were Carleton Watkins and Eadweard Muybridge.

In Europe, Charles Marville documented the streets of old Paris (1864); Thomas Annan did the same in Glasgow, Scotland (1868); and Briton John Thompson traveled to the Orient, producing the four-volume *Illustrations of China and Its People*, published in 1873. Other notable European wet-plate artists included Carlo Ponti in Italy, Charles Clifford in Spain, Gustave Le Gray in France, and Herman Crone in Germany.

Among the thousands of photographers who

used the albumen print process, only a few names are truly deserving of the title "artist." These individuals knew how to make use of camera angles, lighting, and artistic poses to create superb documentary and allegorical scenes and portraits.

In the portrait field, Julia Margaret Cameron was unsurpassed. Using a soft focus and unusual lighting styles, Cameron created photographs that gave the appearance of fine black-and-white paintings. Cameron was born in England in 1815 and took up photography relatively late in life. Most of her work was produced between 1865 and 1875.

Best known among allegorical photographers of the period were British photographers Oscar Gustave Rejlander and Henry Peach Robinson. Rejlander (active in the 1850s through the 1870s) produced complicated scenes, using many models, by photographing small groups and then printing several negatives onto one print (combination printing). He was a vocal advocate of photography as an art.

Robinson's approach followed closely that of Rejlander. Robinson's famous combination print, the controversial "Fading Away" (1858), required five separate negatives to create the image of a dying girl and her bereaved family. Robinson believed that any manipulation the photographer wished to use in order to achieve the desired results was acceptable.

Even though a "dry plate" was introduced as early as 1864, it took until the late 1870s to produce a dry-plate system that could compete with the collodion wet-plate process. At the same time, production of gelatin emulsion paper marked the beginning of the end for albumen prints. Still, it would take more than 20 years for the transition to take place. The wet plate-albumen print marriage had been a long and solid one, and most of the photographers who used these processes remained loyal to the end.

The Wet Plate-Albumen Print Process

The collodion wet-plate negative was used in the production of a number of photographic variants based primarily on mounting styles. (These processes are discussed in the appropriate chapters.) However, from the wet plate negative's early years, the standard objective was the creation of a contact print on albumen paper. When a large print was desired, a large camera and plate were used. These bulky, often massive cameras were commonly carried on expeditions to the American west and used by European travel and art photographers.

The traveling photographer required a portable system which would include a large wet-plate camera; a collection of clean and well protected glass plates; bottles of collodion and chemicals; various trays and utensils; and some sort of darkroom (a wagon for some, a tent for most). While most of the printing was done back at the photographer's place of business, he or she might wish to bring along some paper and chemicals to produce presentation prints for the locals. If the use of a wagon was impractical, all of this equipment was carried by mule or horse. At each destination, the camera was set up and the darkroom and chemicals prepared for use. With the camera positioned and focused, the photographer poured a small amount of collodion onto a glass plate. When the sticky liquid reached the edges, the excess was carefully drained back into the bottle. The plate was then quickly taken to the tent or wagon darkroom to be sensitized in a waiting tray of silver nitrate. Still dripping, it was then placed in a shield and rushed to the camera for exposure.

For scenic views, a lens with a small aperture was used to produce a wider depth of field. This meant lengthy exposure times were required, even in bright sunlight. Although the plate could be cleaned and used again, it was important for a photographer to be well-versed in determining required exposures to avoid wasting time on retakes.

After the exposure was made, the plate was quickly taken back to the tent or wagon darkroom for development in pyrogallic acid. After being fixed in hypo solution, the finished negative was left to dry in a dust-free area, then placed back in the plate transport case.

For the most part, prints of these negatives were made upon the photographer's return, in an outdoor print rack and a standard darkroom. After 1872, albumenized paper could be purchased presensitized and ready for use.

Fig. 6-4. Yosemite Valley by Carleton Watkins, albumen print.

One of a group of three mammoth prints of Yosemite by Watkins that sold at auction in 1998 for $2,070, the lot. (Courtesy of Swann Galleries, Inc.)

Prior to that date, photographers purchased the paper in reams, cut the sheets to size, and sensitized them in a silver nitrate bath. When necessary, sensitized paper could be prepared one or two days in advance, but best results were achieved with freshly sensitized paper.

To make a print, the collodion negative was placed in direct contact with a sheet of the sensitized paper and locked in a printing frame. The frame was then taken to an area where it could receive exposure to direct sunlight for a period of 10 to 30 minutes. This process was carefully monitored so that the print would achieve the proper degree of darkening before being taken in for toning and fixing procedures.

While several different toning methods were used, the one most commonly practiced was a gold chloride-alkaline bath. This process produced rich, purplish-brown tones in the finished image. After toning, the albumen print was fixed in hypo solution, rinsed, and mounted. Because albumen paper was thin and subject to curling, prints were almost always mounted on cardboard using a carefully applied starch or flour paste. Even during these early years of photography, it was known that ordinary glues were harmful to the long-term stability of an image.

As the twentieth century approached, many improvements were made to the wet-plate albumen-print process, mostly to refine the system and make it more convenient. On the whole, however, the basic operation remained unchanged until the advent of gelatin bromide technology at the turn of the century.

Collecting the Albumen Print

No other category of nineteenth-century images provides a larger base of availability than albumen prints. Between 1850 and 1900,

millions of images were produced by portrait artists, itinerants, and amateurs. Nearly every subject one can imagine has been documented by the albumen print.

For the purpose of this chapter, we confine ourselves to all albumen prints *not* mounted in the style of the card photograph (i.e., prints that do not fall into the categories of carte de visite, cabinet card, or stereograph). Albumen prints ranged in size from 1" x 1" to 20" x 24" or larger. These prints were either mounted in

Fig. 6-5. White Women in an Opium Den, San Francisco, 1892, by I. W. Taber, albumen print.

An unusually candid image of what would have been a shocking subject in the 1890s. Important historical prints can occasionally be found mixed with ordinary photographs at flea markets and estate sales. These images may then bring premium prices at sale or auction. (Collection of Joseph T. Silva)

albums, "tipped-in" to books, or attached to cardboard mounts. Examples can be found at flea markets and antique stores and through dealers and auction houses on a regular basis. Almost every home has at least a few albumen prints in the family album or picture box.

Albumen prints usually display some degree of deterioration in the form of fading and yellowing (especially near the edges), and also stains and "foxing" (brown spots). Because most albumen prints were toned, the dark areas of the image are almost always brown or purplish in color, although gray-blacks are not uncommon.

What to look for

The value of an albumen print is often highly affected by the identification of the photographer. Prints bringing high prices are almost always quality examples by well-known artists. Often these prints were produced as part of a series, with the number, series title, and photographer's credit embossed or printed on the print or mount. Occasionally an image without a credit can be attributed to a specific photographer by comparison to other works of a similar type, subject, and/or photographic style.

Fig. 6-6. Man with Chair, albumen print.

A wide variety of subjects can be found as albumen prints. Ordinary portraits seldom have value beyond being examples of period clothing and settings. During the latter part of the century, greater numbers of amateur photographers were producing outdoor views and portraits. (Collection of the author)

Availability/Value Classifications

The common albumen print ($5 to $50)

Millions of images of homes, businesses, towns, people, and animals, produced by both professionals and amateurs, make up 97 percent of the available base of albumen prints and are mostly considered *common*. A collector may be drawn to a particular image because he or she finds some personal connection or aesthetic appeal. In recent years, even these common images have become considerably more collectible, due primarily to a recognition of their historical documentary value. Collectors should expect values in this category to continue to rise.

Examples of recent sales:

8" x 10" portrait of mother and child, antique shop, $7

12" x 16" family portrait featuring sixteen family members, antique shop, $15

6" x 8" portrait of couple; possible wedding photo, dealer, $20

4" x 5" portrait of man in uniform, late 19th century, antique shop, $25

7" x 9" view of nice clapboard house and garden, antique shop, $25

7" x 9" view of beach/ocean scene, dealer, $35

6" x 8" view of unknown town, dealer, $40

8" x 10" portrait of man with shotgun and dog, dealer, $48

Scrap book containing 25 small prints of travel scenes, antique shop, $50

The uncommon albumen print ($50 to $250)

While the *uncommon* albumen image makes up only about 2 percent of the available base, it must be remembered that the overall base is very large. Included in this category are "collectible" images such as those containing horse-drawn carriages, Indians or blacks, people in costume or uniform, and identifiable businesses, streets, towns, etc. Certain "mass-produced" images by Francis Frith, George Washington Wilson, Alexander Gardner, and others can occasionally be found in the under-$100 price range. Portraiture (other than cartes or cabinets) by Nadar, Lewis Carroll, and Antoine Salomon can also be found from time to time.

Examples of recent sales:

8" x 10" portrait of unknown military group, late 19th century, dealer, $55

11" x 14" mass-produced image of cathedral, marked Frith's Series, dealer, $60

6" x 8" view of carriage containing 6 men; picket fence in background, dealer, $75

Fig. 6-7. Chat with the Keeper by Henry Peach Robinson, hand-colored albumen print.

One of the better known allegorical photographers, Robinson believed in doing whatever was necessary to achieve artistic results, including using retouching and overlaying multiple negatives. This print sold at auction in 1998 for $1,725. (Courtesy of Swann Galleries, Inc.)

7" x 9" "portrait" of high-masted sailing ship,
    by Wilton, auction, $150

8" x 10" view of Colorado mining camp,
    by Harlan, auction, $185

7" x 9" view of impressive Greek revival school
    building, auction, $225

6" x 8" view of Illinois town Main Street, dealer,
    $240

The rare albumen print
($250 to $2,500)

Rare albumen prints are a great starting place
for the investor in nineteenth-century photography. Quality works by major photographers are
now bringing $500+ at auction, with values stead-
ily increasing. Recent sales by Swann Galleries and
Sotheby's included many superb works by Americans O'Sullivan, Gardner, Barnard, Jackson, and
Muybridge and European artists John Thomson,
Francis Frith, and James Anderson.

Examples of recent sales:
8" x 11" view of the Sentinel-Yosemite,
    by Watkins, auction, $345

10" x 14" print of ship being unloaded, by Bell,
    auction, $373

9" x 12" view of Arizona pueblo ruins, by Hillers,
    auction, $450

14" x 17" tinted view of Moscow, by Nabholz,
    auction, $1,035

Nine 3" x 5" prints of Middle East subjects,
    by Frith, auction, $1,265

6" x 8" portrait of Lincoln and son Tad,
    by Gardner, auction, $1,380

6" x 8" view of Black farm workers with wagon
    and cabin, by Moore, auction, $2,070

11" x 14" view of Italian street, by Marville,
    auction, $2,185

The premium albumen print
($2,500 and up)

This category consists primarily of
books illustrated with original prints, rare
series, and unique portraits. From an investment point of view, these items could easily
double in value by the time offerings of this
type are made again.

Examples of past sales:
Large print, group of Navajo in camp from
    Wheeler Survey series, O'Sullivan,
    auction, $3,520

Portfolio book with 14 large prints of Middle East
    subjects, auction, by Frith, $6,820

Portrait of Robert E. Lee, by Brady, auction,
    $10,450.

Above all the talk of art and investment
value, there is one often-forgotten factor
concerning the albumen print. Spanning the
second half of the nineteenth century, it documented 50 important years of world history. The
changes in fashion, architecture, transportation,
and lifestyle were all etched in silver on albumen.
Despite their perceived value (or lack thereof),
these early paper prints should be preserved and
studied as the historical artifacts they are.

CHAPTER 7
CARTE DE VISTE

carte de vis 'ite: An albumen print measuring 2-1/2" by 3-1/2" mounted to a card measuring 2-1/2" by 4". Popularized by André-Adolphe-Eugène Disdéri (France).

Introduced	1854
Peak years	1859-1866
Waned	1870-1905

History of the Carte de Visite

While the exact origins of cartes de visite are unknown, it is a fact that they did not come into extensive use until their introduction by Frenchman André-Adolphe-Eugène Disdéri in 1854. Disdéri had devised a rotating camera back which, using the recently invented collodion wet plate, could produce eight individually exposed images on a single negative. After printing on albumen paper, the images were cut apart and glued to calling card-sized mounts. These tiny portraits were left by visiting friends, inspiring the name *carte de visite* (French for "visiting card").

During the early years (1854 to 1857), the "carte" was popular on a limited basis throughout Europe. By 1858, it had spread to America, and by 1860, photographers around the world were producing more cartes de visite than any other type of photograph. In August of that year, John Mayall, an American working in England, advanced the notoriety of the carte de visite when he published 60,000 sets of his Royal Family album (Queen Victoria herself was an avid carte collector).

Former daguerreotypist Charles D. Fredricks was one of the earliest promoters of the carte de visite in America, having introduced the new format in his gallery as early as 1859. During the years 1860 to 1865, Americans learned all too well the ability of the photograph to capture and hold a memory. The carte de visite portrayed sons and fathers gone to war, wives and children left behind, and the visages of heroes, both alive and fallen. Photography was so popular during the Civil War that a special revenue bill was passed requiring an additional tax stamp to be affixed to photographs sent through the mail (see Chapter 11).

Fig. 7-1. Fig. 7-2. Napoleon III by Disderi.

 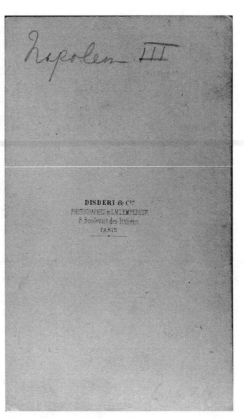

Disderi has been credited with introducing the carte de visite in 1854. One of the first uses of the carte de visite was to produce images of royalty in quantity for sale to the public. (Courtesy of the Motzenbecker Collection)

Between 1861 and 1865, 15 patents were issued for albums to hold the new card photographs. Generally, they contained cardboard pages with slots into which the carte was inserted on each side, back to back. The album covers were usually made of cloth or embossed leather, with numerous adornments (painted insets, porcelain knobs, brass and sometimes gold latches). This style of album would remain popular well into the next century.

A study of existing carte de visite albums indicates that an etiquette developed concerning the arrangement of images in the Victorian album. Many began with the U.S. president and various celebrities of the day, followed by autographed images of friends and business associates, then family pictures. At the end of the album were travel views, pictures of European royalty (often Queen Victoria), and, finally, images of various works of art.

The largest photographic supplier in the United States, Edward Anthony, was among the first to realize the potential of mass-produced "collector" cartes. Negatives of famous people and places were purchased from various amateur and professional photographers for publication as cartes de visite. Among the primary supplier of celebrity portraits was Mathew Brady. His images of Jenny Lind, Tom Thumb, President Lincoln, and various Civil War personages were as popular then as they are with collectors today. Other important portrait artists from the daguerreotype era remained popular as carte de visite photographers. Samuel Broadbent, John Whipple, Abraham Bogardus, and Southworth and Hawes all maintained busy carte studios.

During the 1870s and 1880s, Napoleon Sarony became America's premier celebrity photographer, producing thousands of imaginative portraits of leading actors and performers on both the carte de visite and the cabinet card.

Fig. 7-3. Queen Victoria by W. & D. Downey.

As well as being a popular subject of card photographs, Victoria was an avid collector of cartes de visite. This image bears a rare copyright notification—generally, cartes of famous people and places were freely copied and distributed by other photographers. (Courtesy of the Motzenbecker Collection)

Fig. 7-4. Fig. 7-5. Senator David C. Broderick, by Mathew Brady.

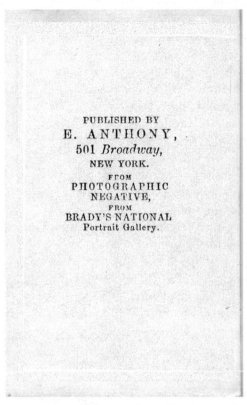

Collectors often spend hours searching through stacks of cartes looking for the Brady backmark. While large numbers of Brady images were distributed by Edward Anthony & Co. in the mid-to-late 1800s, collector demand makes them difficult to find in today's market. (Collection of Joseph T. Silva)

The distinctive signature of Sarony imprinted on the mount often means that the sitter was someone of importance. The practice of imprinting the photographer's signature on the mount was copied by many, including Sarony's imitative protégé, Mora, who also photographed stage celebrities and was famous for his elaborate backgrounds and accessories.

A number of French portrait photographers were also well known for their cartes de visite. Etienne Carjat, Reutlinger, and Nadar all produced superb card photographs, as did the originator of the format, Disdéri. A number of French firms published mass-produced cartes of architecture and artwork.

In England, former daguerreotypists Antoine Claudet and John Mayall took up the carte de visite with great success. Also important among British carte producers were Jabez

Hughes, William Kilburn, Camille Silvy, and the firms of Elliot & Fry, Hill & Sanders, Nigretti & Zambra, and Maull and Polybank.

You will notice that nearly all the above names appear again in reference to the cabinet card and the stereograph. Most firms produced all three formats and mass-produced images for each style of mount.

The tintype as carte de visite

With the advent of the American Civil War, demand was high for inexpensive portraits that were easy to carry or mail. The carte de visite fit that description perfectly. In order to compete, tintypists began to produce small "gem" portraits which could be placed in carte de visite-sized sleeves. (Prior to this time, tintypes had always been sold in standard plate sizes as cased images.)

Fig. 7-6. Charles Albert Fechter, actor, by Sarony.

SARONY, *Fechter* 680 BROADWAY.

Fig. 7-7. Edward Hugh Sothern as Lord Dundreary, by Gurney and Son.

GURNEY & SON, FIFTH AVE. N. Y.

Actors of the 19th century used cartes de visite much as today's actors use head shots and zed sheets. And the best actors chose only the best photographers. The names Sarony or Gurney on a carte de visite usually mean the subject was someone of stature or fame. (Collection of Kathleen Fehr)

A multi-lens camera with a rotating back, patented by Simon Wing in 1860, was capable of producing large numbers of "gems" on a single plate. Wing also introduced a mounting card with an oval window cutout to contain the tiny portraits. Also popular were the Potter's Patent sleeves with embossed patterns, and small albums that held 100 or more images.

After the war, larger tintypes were produced for carte de visite sleeves with larger openings. Although use of the tintype for portraiture declined in the late 1870s, tins were made in the carte format by beach and boardwalk photographers until the early 1900s.

If a complete directory of carte de visite photographers was ever published, it would be a massive volume including hundreds of thousands of entries from the Americas, Europe, Asia, and even the South Pacific. While production of the carte was reduced by the introduction of cabinet cards in 1866, large quantities continued to be made by photographers worldwide until just after the turn of the century.

The Carte de Visite Process

Of paramount importance to the carte de visite process was the multi-lens camera with repeating back. Using a "four tube" camera (four lenses), the photographer could produce four separate exposures on one-half of the plate, then shift the back and take four more exposures on the other half. With the option of either uncapping all four lenses at once or each one individually, the resulting negative could contain either eight nearly identical images or eight separate poses. Regardless of how the exposures were made, they had to be done quickly, because the sensitivity of the collodion wet plate was steadily changing as the coating began to dry.

Fig. 7-8. Tintypes as Cartes de Visite.

Tintypes in a variety of sizes were inserted into carte-sized sleeves so that they could be easily carried or stored in albums. Potters Patent sleeves had embossed patterns around the opening, and those with patriotic designs were very popular during the civil war. (Collection of the author)

Fig. 7-9. Scottish Soldier.

Cartes with foreign subjects are frequently found in American albums. Those that show eye-catching clothing or accessories, and especially those related to the military or other occupations, are highly collectible. (Courtesy of the Motzenbecker Collection)

After the full-plate negative containing eight 2-1/2" x 3-1/2" images was developed, it was contact-printed onto a freshly sensitized sheet of albumen paper. Larger galleries had rooftop printing racks that could be adjusted to the angle of the sun. Assistants were hired to periodically examine the prints for proper image intensity. When intensity was judged to be correct, the print was taken inside to be fixed and toned. Then the individual prints were cut apart, trimmed, and mounted to the card mounts (2-1/2" x 4"). As with brass mats, preservers, and other "adornments" of nineteenth-century photography, early cards were very plain, becoming constantly more elaborate as the years passed.

After the initial printing, the original negative was usually kept on file by the photographer for future reorders. Many extant cartes have a number penciled on the back which corresponded to the file number on the original negative.

Sitting for a carte de visite portrait was not much different from previous sitting processes except that the carte sitter was surrounded by many elaborate "furnishings." Pillars, pedestals, ornate velvet settees, elegant draperies, and detailed painted backdrops were all tools of the trade for a carte photographer. The ever-present head rest was always hiding somewhere, and its "third foot" often made an appearance in standing portraits.

By the 1870s, accessories were varied and abundant, almost to the point of absurdity. Rustic gates and fences, rowboats, wishing wells, a jungle of plants and flowers, and even snow adorned the studio setting.

Fig. 7-10. The Hunters.

Elaborate indoor scenery became popular for backdrops during the latter part of the 19th century. In this case, the woodsy backdrop and log props seem very appropriate for two boys in hunting garb, holding shotguns. (Courtesy of the Motzenbecker Collection)

Fig. 7-11. Postmortem of Baby.

Although some may find postmortems a bit morbid, they play an important role in the history of photography. In most cases, the person being photographed in death had never been photographed in life. This was a final opportunity to record what that person looked like before the grave. Postmortems in all image types are highly sought after by collectors. (Courtesy of the Motzenbecker Collection)

The carte de visite gallery also provided a number of services other than standard portraiture. Copies were made of daguerreotypes and other early images, as well as paintings and artwork. Most major galleries carried a line of commercially produced cartes which could be added to an album to impress friends. These included portraits of celebrities, foreign scenes, famous landmarks, works of art, etc.

The carte de visite was also the first commercially viable method of photographing the various individual members of groups, such as university faculty, senators and representatives, or members of clubs. Like the ambrotype before it, the carte de visite was even used for "mug shots."

When you understand the difficulties in producing images by the wet-plate process, you realize that it was no small effort that produced the millions of cartes de visite made from 1860 to 1900 and that it is no small miracle that millions of superb examples still exist in reasonably good condition. The carte de visite is also a tribute to the men whose separate visions were combined in its conception: Frederick Scott Archer (collodion negatives), Louis-Désiré Blanquart-Evrard (albumen paper), and André-Adolphe-Eugène Disdéri (card photographs).

Collecting Cartes de Visite

More people collect the carte de visite than any other form of photography. Carte images are widely available at flea markets, estate sales, and antique shops at very reasonable prices.

Fig. 7-12. California Gold Miner by William Shew.

The Shew brothers (William, Myron, Jacob, Trueman) came to San Francisco during the Gold Rush as daguerreotypists and William maintained a successful photography business there for many years. Collectors now watch diligently for the highly collectible Shew backmark. (Collection of John McWilliams)

Woman with smiling baby, 1/4-plate daguerreotype in passe-partout frame Under most circumstances, the halo of tarnish that sometimes encroaches on a daguerreotype image is simply annoying. In this case, it seems to provide a "time-tunnel" through which a 140-year-old Shirley Temple look-alike smiles sweetly. (Collection of the author.)

Pretty woman with a pink bow, 1/6-plate daguerreotype. (Collection of William Dunniway)

The Mascher view, first introduced in 1852, became the standard for mounting and viewing daguerreian stereo portraits. (Collection of the author.)

Nevada miners, half-plate ambrotype. (Collection of Joseph T. Silva)

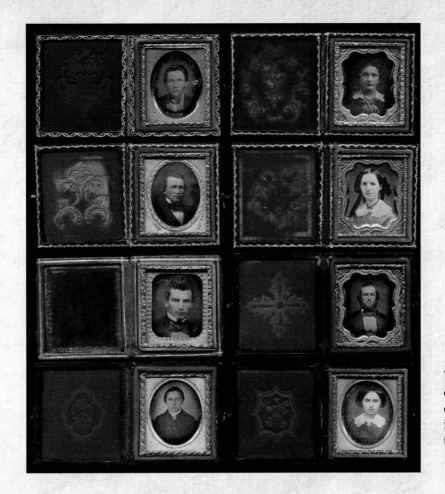

Tiny faces, a collection of 1/16-plate daguerreotype images. (Collection of the author.)

Tiny cases, a collection of 1/16-plate image cases. (Collection of the author.)

A unique and beautiful enameled case in the style of cloisonné. (Courtesy of Paul K. Berg)

Hand colored carte de visite with colorist's label on verso. (Courtesy of the Motzenbecker Collection)

Hand painted carte de visite album cover. (Collection of Kathleen Fehr)

◄◄ Hose Reel Co., Watsonville, California, hand-colored albumen print. (Collection of Joseph T. Silva)

CROWNED QUEEN OF THE MAY.

◄◄ A richly colored stereograph, possibly printed using the collotype process. (Courtesy of the Motzenbecker collection)

➤➤ **Top, Center, and Bottom:** Panorama de Paris, French tissue stereograph. By painting the back of the photograph then viewing it by transmitted light, the effect of a colored scene could be achieved. A "tissue" attached to the back of the stereograph helped to diffuse the light. (Collection of the author)

Charles B. Mitchell, 9th
Kentucky Infantry, C.S.A.
(Courtesy of William
Dunniway, Collection of
Sam E. Young)

Young Union
Cavalryman, 1/4-plate
ambrotype. (Collection
of D. J. Knowles)

Just as the carte was the "poor man's portrait" in the nineteenth century, it is now the poor man's collectible, with collectible examples going for as little as $5.

Fig. 7-14. Black man in coat and cap.

(Courtesy of the Motzenbecker Collection)

Fig. 7-15. Boy with logging tools.

Highly collectible images of this type can often be found among ordinary images in family albums. One such image is often worth the cost of the entire album. (Courtesy of the Motzenbecker Collection)

Fig. 7-13. Dog on stool by Ramshaw.

What to look for

Carte de visite collectors are usually subject collectors. They spend endless weekends searching through dusty boxes and albums for that elusive carte of a little girl holding a doll, or a nameless Civil War soldier. Some collect portraits of famous people, just as the Victorians did 100 years ago. Still others are watching for the famous imprints of Brady, Nadar, Sarony, Disdéri, etc. While thousands of these cartes exist, their popularity as a collector's item makes them hard to find, and therefore valuable.

(Courtesy of the Motzenbecker Collection)

Generally speaking, for a carte de visite image to attain more than *uncommon* status, it must have significant historical value and/or be appreciable as an artistic piece. Historical images could be "original" portraits of politicians, celebrities, and royalty or documentary views of historical events and landmarks. Artistic cartes are "original" portraits and allegorical views by Cameron, Rejlander, Robinson, Carroll, and so on. *Original* in this context means "as produced by the photographer or his publisher" (that is, not a pirated copy).

Fig. 7-16. The Apparition.

(Courtesy of the Motzenbecker Collection)

Fig. 7-17. Corset Maker.

Fig. 7-18. Telegrapher.

Because of their small size, it is often easy to miss elements within a carte de visite that greatly increase the collectibility. What appears as a faded area may be a ghostly apparition. The pieces of cloth in someone's hand or a device on the table may point to that person's occupation. (Collection of D. J. Knowles)

(Courtesy of the Motzenbecker Collection)

Availability/Value Classifications

The common carte de visite ($1 to $10)

The *common* carte is a portrait whose value relies solely upon its antiquity and inner charm (if any). It is an accurate record of fashion and style, as well as nineteenth-century class structures. All carte-de-visite portraits should be examined for signatures or notations which identify the subject. This is especially true of cartes in albums, where the backs of the cards are not visible. One such album, purchased by the author some years back for $15, contained 35 seemingly common cartes. When the portraits were removed and examined, the backs were found to contain Civil War period tax stamps and notations identifying the subjects as the family of U.S. General George McClellan.

Common cartes de visite are still quite readily available at $3 to $5 each. The collector should be aware that the prices of common cartes   de visite vary widely among sellers and are often overpriced, especially in antique shops. The best prices can often be had by buying complete albums. Occasionally, such albums contain one or two images that are worth the price of the album.

Examples of recent sales:

Loose group of 25 ordinary portraits, antique shop, $30 ($1.20 per image)

Album containing 85 cartes and cdv-sized tintypes, dealer, $125 ($1.47 per image)

Portrait of pretty little girl holding hand-tinted rose, antique shop, $5

Portrait of young man, Civil War era stamp on verso, antique shop, $5

Still life of marble statue of Shakespeare, antique shop, $5

Portrait of man in top hat, holding cane and cigar, dealer, $7

View of unknown house with people standing on porch, antique shop, $10

Portrait of little girl holding doll, dealer, $10

The uncommon carte de visite ($10 to $500)

Uncommon cartes are the "collectibles," that make up around 15 percent of the available base. On the lower end of the value range are theatrical subjects, and children with toys or pets. In the mid-to-upper range are scenics, occupational portraits, images of musicians and bands, death portraits, historical subjects, and ethnic images.

Certain carte de visite subjects can be found in nearly every price range, depending on specifics of the individual piece. These subjects include artwork and architecture, celebrities, military, and works by well-known photographers. Collectible cartes which do not contain a photographer's imprint are probably pirated, and pirated prints are worth considerably less than originals.

Examples of recent sales:

Portrait of unidentified man, Anthony backmark, dealer, $10

CDV of Lincoln lithograph portrait, dealer, $25

Portrait of statesman W. H. Seward, Anthony backmark, auction, $25

Tom Thumb and two female "little people," Anthony backmark, auction, $30

Portrait of Longfellow, by Sarony, auction, $35

Still life of world globe sitting on table, dealer, $35

Portrait of dog identified as "Snip Gordon," auction, $50

View identified as "Campbellite Church at Danville, Cala.," auction, $60

Overview of Pennsylvania town, by Harner & Harding, auction, $65

Black man standing by posing chair, auction, $70

Three women in maid uniforms with dishes, broom, etc., auction, $70

Postmortem of elderly black man, auction, $95

Nude woman in demure pose, dealer, $100

Bird's eye view of Red Wing, Minnesota, auction, $100

Portrait of two young boys, one white, one Indian, with bows & arrows, auction, $325

Three CDV's of American Indians, auction, $1,150 ($383 each)

Fig. 7-19. Lotta Crabtree.

(Collection of the Author)

The value of some cartes de visite is sometimes difficult to ascertain. Lotta Crabtree was a well-know actress of the mid-19th century who, like Marilyn Monroe in this century, has endeared herself to many people who know her only from her biography and who never pass up the chance to purchase an original photo of her. And, almost any image of a Native American will draw interest from collectors who specialize in that field. Accordingly, both the below images have brought impressive prices despite the fact that they were produced in large quantity. (Collection of the author.)

Fig. 7-20. Indian Woman.

Fig. 7-21. Backmark for 7-20.

CAN-KU WAS-TE WIN, (Good Road Woman.)

A SIOUX BEAUTY.

Whitney's Gallery,   St. Paul, Minn.

The rare carte de visite ($500 to $1,000, including albums)

Although they represent only about 5 percent of the available base, *rare* cartes and albums are not difficult to locate through dealers or auctions. Individual examples are usually unique or limited-production celebrity portraits or photographic art. *Rare* carte de visite albums are often filled with images of celebrities, politicians, royalty, famous landmarks, artworks, and so on, collected by wealthy Victorians for prominent display in the parlor.

Fig. 7-22. Linking the Rails at Promontory by Savage & Attenger.

This rare carte contains a less common view of the famous "driving of the golden spike."
(Collection of Jerry Mack)

Fig. 7-23. Sarah Bernhardt by Nadar.

A rare, early image of this famous actress, this carte de visite sold at auction in 1998 for $3,450. (Courtesy of Swan Galleries, Inc.)

Examples of recent sales:

Group portrait, seated white man surrounded by black family, dealer, $500

Album containing 28 images of famous Americans, most Anthony backmarks, dealer, $625 lot

Pornographic image of man and two women, dealer, $800

Portrait of Sarah Bernhardt in costume, by Sarony, dealer, $850

Portrait of Mrs. Lincoln with "ghost" of Abe over shoulder, auction, $920

The premium carte de visite
($1,000 and up, including albums)

Occasionally an individual carte will bring in excess of $1,000. Usually it is a unique photograph of a historical subject, often accompanied by an autograph or other important historical papers.

Examples of recent sales:

Portrait of black woman identified as Sojourner Truth, auction, $1,150

Buckskin-clad frontiersman posed with scalps, auction, $2,005

CDV's of President Lincoln, his tomb, and a painting of the conspirators, $2,760 lot

Dating the Carte de Visite

A number of characteristics of the carte de visite mount can be used as an aid in determining the approximate date of the image it contains. Pre-Civil War cartes were usually attached to thin, unadorned, white or cream-colored card mounts with square corners. From about 1860 to 1868, the images were attached to the same thin cardboard stock with square corners but usually with one or two gold or red lines imprinted as a border. After 1863, some cards were imprinted with a representation of an oval picture frame into which the image was glued.

After 1869, a thicker card was used, and after 1871, the corners were rounded. Various colored card mounts were introduced around 1873, and by 1875, beveled edges trimmed in gilt were in use. By 1880, the card stock was thick and sturdy, and rich, dark colors were common. The backs of these cards contained the photographer's logo, incorporated into elabo-rately printed designs. In 1890, cards were again made thicker, with scalloped or other fancy edges.

It is always a treat for the collector to discover a date written on the back of the card by some thoughtful ancestor; however, this is the exception, rather than the rule. By using the above guidelines, a collector can arrive at an approximate production date, adding to the value and interest of the image. With collecting experience, the recognition of time periods becomes second nature.

Documentation and Storage

Like the cased image, the carte de visite has various elements which should be documented. This is especially important if the card is contained in an album where frequent removal and insertion can be harmful. Notations should be made as to the dimensions and thickness of the mount and whether the corners are rounded or square. The color of the front and back, as well as the texture and trimwork, are also important. The photographer's name and address should be documented and the logo (if any) described. Finally, any markings, attachments, or written notations should be recorded and a simple description of the image given. Rarely can the entire history of an image, including previous owners, be determined. If such a provenance is available for an image, the information is extremely important and should be kept.

Like all paper images, the carte de visite is susceptible to excessive heat and moisture, oils, acids, and fading. Since even many museums and archives cannot afford proper photographic storage facilities, it is enough to say that collectors should do the best they can to avoid these dangers. Loose cartes are best kept in Mylar

Fig. 7-25. Billie Robinson, Banjo Player by W. D. Bennett.

Fig. 7-26. Verso of 7-25.

This rare carte de visite of a black banjo player is not only identified, the back contains a Civil War-era 2c proprietary stamp and bears the date 1864. Such an image would bring a premium price at sale or auction. (Collection of Joseph Silva)

Fig. 7-27. Native American Carte.

This somewhat informal portrait of two young Indians meets the requirements of a premium carte de visite–the subject matter is unusual and in high demand, and the piece itself is in excellent condition. (Collection of D. J. Knowles)

sleeves or pages. Images in original albums can be given some degree of protection by the insertion of acid-free paper between the pages. If you must write on any paper image or its mount, use a soft lead pencil and write lightly, near the edge. Never use ink on any photograph, old or new.

The carte de visite appears to provide the collector with a seemingly endless supply of undiscovered treasures. In fact, the value and historical importance of this photographic medium is overlooked for just that reason. Thousands of these "old photos" are ruined annually by mishandling and improper storage. It is important for those who are interested in the preservation of photography and of our heritage to include the carte de visite in collection and preservation efforts.

Fig. 7-29. Tintype copy of a picture, mounted as a carte de visite.

(Collection of the author.)

Fig. 7-30. Man with Salvation Army badge.

Fig. 7-28. Log Sawing Machine.

Horizontal cartes are usually scenic images of homes, towns, or "activities." Therefore, most are highly collectible.
(Courtesy of the Motzenbecker Collection)

(Collection of Gregory Fried)

Fig. 7-32. Railroad Surveyors in Utah by Savage & Ottenger.

(Collection of Jerry Mack)

Fig. 7-31. Bird on a perch.

(Collection of Jerry Mack)

Fig. 7-33. View of Bridge by J. H. Crawford.

(Collection of Jerry Mack)

CHAPTER 8

CABINET CARDS

cabinet card: A photographic print measuring 4" x 5-1/2" attached to a cardboard mount 4-1/4" x 6-1/2". Popularized by Windsor & Bridge (Britain).

Introduced   1863
Peak years   1870-1900
Waned   1905-1920

History of the Cabinet Card

The early history of the cabinet card and specifics of the process are closely related to those of the carte de visite. Also, the value of collectible cabinet cards is determined in a similar manner. Therefore, a thorough study of both chapters is advised.

Despite the great success of the carte de visite during the early 1860s and its continued popularity thereafter, demand was high for a new larger type of portrait which could be made for a reasonable price. Whole-plate and "imperial photographs" (see Glossary) were too costly to produce in volume, and they required framing. The public had quickly become accustomed to the family album, but the tiny cartes just seemed too small (Victorians were used to doing everything in a big way).

The answer came, not from the French this time, but from the London studios of Windsor & Bridge. In 1863, Windsor & Bridge announced a new large card photograph (four

Fig. 8-1. Native American with Flag.

After several decades of collecting four-inch cartes de visite, Victorian America was thrilled with the clarity and detail of the larger cabinet card. Unusual subjects such as this one were highly prized then and now. (Collection of Jelena McWilliams)

Fig. 8-2. Women in Fake Snow.

The large size of the cabinet card seemed to cry out for more things to be placed in the scene—more background, and more props. (Collection of Kathleen Fehr)

times larger than the carte) consisting of a 4" x 5-1/2" albumen print on a 4-1/4" x 6-1/2" heavy cardboard mount. Prior to the production of albums for the new format, the large cards were prominently displayed in the drawing room cabinet, thus inspiring the name *cabinet card.*

Fig. 8-3. Lotta Crabtree.

As with the carte de visite, photographers produced images of celebrities in quantity for sale to the public, and they are still in demand today. (Collection of the author.)

Photographers were delighted with the new images, which were produced in pairs on a full-plate negative. Most galleries continued to offer the carte de visite, giving the customer a choice of sizes, and, as the cabinet card became more popular, larger albums were created with pages to accommodate both formats.

As usual, American photographers waited for the innovation to prove itself before taking up the new format in 1866. Names that were already known for their cartes de visite (Sarony, Mora, Gurney, and so on) quickly became known for their carefully posed, well-accessorized, and deftly retouched cabinet portraits.

Retouching was an important feature of the cabinet card process. The large negative could be carefully doctored by the artist to eliminate wrinkles, blemishes, and stray strands of hair, as well as to correct any photographic defects. The art of photography, which upon its conception had inspired the quote "from this day painting is dead," now relied on the painter's craft as an integral component of its newest process.

The practice of including various accessories and backgrounds in a portrait reached almost absurd proportions in cabinet card studios. Photographers felt that this new large format could handle elaborately detailed sets. To us, in the twentieth century, these settings appear quite gaudy and unnecessarily ornate. However, contemporary photographs of Victorian homes show that this was very much the style of the period.

Beginning in the late 1880s, a declining interest in carte and cabinet card portraiture prompted an increase in the production of art, travel, and celebrity images for sale to the public. However, the discovery and subsquent development of the half-tone printing process brought the same subjects to the readers of books, magazines, and newspapers. By the turn of the century, photomechanized printing would effect the demise of commercially produced card photographs. After 1900, only stereographs would continue to use mass-produced photographic images in their manufacture.

Cabinet card portraiture continued to receive moderate use until the beginning of World War I. By that time, the wet-plate process was a thing of the past, albumen paper had been replaced by gelatin-silver, and modern enlarging techniques made full-size framable portraits the format of the twentieth century.

Fig. 8-4. Children with sheep.

This image may have been taken specifically for a family, but more likely it was produced in quantity as an "endearing" collectible image—a value it retains today. (Courtesy of the Motzenbecker Collection)

The Cabinet Card Process

Cabinet cards of the nineteenth century were primarily produced in the same manner as cartes de visite, using a wet-plate negative printed on albumen paper. The major difference was the camera, which, in the production of the cabinet card, was a standard full-plate camera employing twin lenses to produce either two identical prints or two separate poses, side by side on one plate. The negative was often first printed onto factory-sensitized proof paper which required no chemical processing. This print was used by the artist as a guide for retouching the negative, after which a second "improved" print was shown to the sitter. Once the order was taken, multiple prints were produced on standard albumen paper and mounted to the cardboard mounts.

After the introduction of the dry-plate system around 1880, cabinet card photographers used factory-sensitized plates that could be exposed throughout the day, then processed all at once. Even with the advent of gelatin-based papers, albumen prints remained the choice of most cabinet portrait artists until after the turn of the century.

Other processes used in the production of cabinet cards (and, to a lesser degree, cartes de visite) included platinum prints, bromide prints, carbon prints, Velox, mezzotint, and photomechanical prints such as woodbury-types and collotypes.

Collecting the Cabinet Card

Most cabinet cards currently being held in private collections are there because of some personal appeal the image has for the collector, not because of real or perceived monetary value.

Fig. 8-5. Grinning dirty child.

Bruce. THORNBURG, IOWA.

It is difficult to say if this is a little boy or little girl since both wore dresses at this age, but the cherubic quality comes through either way. Such highly collectible cabinet cards can sometimes be found in an album of otherwise ordinary images. (Courtesy of Julie and Dominic Santangelo)

This is not to say that there are no valuable cabinet cards. However, 95 percent of the available market of cabinet cards can be considered to be in the *common* category.

A good example of the prevailing attitude toward cabinet cards can be seen at flea markets and antique shops, where more than half of all albums which originally contained cartes de visite are sold empty because the images have been removed for separate sale. At that same location, however, you will find nearly every cabinet card album filled with its original images.

Because they are from a later time period, cabinet cards do not display the historic look of cartes and other early images. Generally, in comparison to the carte de visite, the cabinet card has a sharper image, a shinier finish, and is in cleaner condition. In short, for the average collector of antiquarian images, the cabinet card is just too new.

It is this attitude which makes the cabinet card one of the best starting places for beginning collectors. The true potential of the cabinet card is just now starting to be recognized. Just as we are looking forward to a new century today, so did the world of the 1880s and 90s.

Fig. 8-6. Man dressed as woman.

Gilbert & Bacon. Nº 40 N EIGHTH ST.

While images of men in "drag" are certainly highly collectible, they are not as rare as you might think. Both actors and actresses of the 19th century donned clothing of the opposite sex for various roles. Cabinet cards of actors in costume are highly sought-after by collectors. (Collection of Gregory Fried)

Fig. 8-7. Fig. 8-8. Advertising Card Photograph.

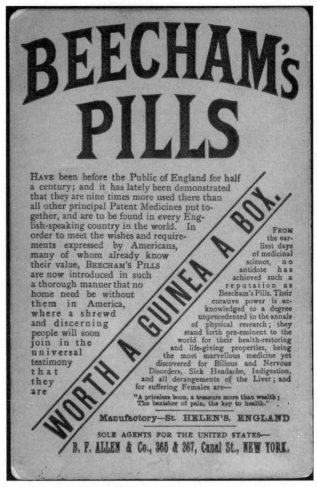

It didn't take advertisers long to realize that the public's appreciation of photographs of celebrities could be used to advantage. Here a cabinet card of President Harrison doubles as an advertisement for Beechham's Pills.
(Courtesy of Julie and Dominic Santangelo)

It was a time of invention, transition, and moreover, a time of affluence and high spirits. The statesman, the thespian, the scientist, the Gibson Girl–feathers and lace and a glimpse of stocking–were kept in elaborate velvet albums to remind future generations of a time when life was a whole lot lighter.

What to look for

The current trend in cabinet-card collecting centers on the photographer and/or unique subjects. Imprints of Sarony, Mora, Nadar, Brady, Disdéri, and others are in great demand. Scenic and documentary cabinets (often identi-

cal to stereograph images) are also in collecting vogue. Early cabinet cards are becoming harder to find, especially those made at or near the end of the Civil War.

Availability/Value Classifications

The common cabinet card (50 cents to $5)

Common cabinet cards are often used to fill fancy albums and/or as conversation pieces. Many are enjoyable as chronicles of fashion and late Victorian gaudery. When looking through stacks of common cabinet cards at flea markets or antique shops, watch for imprints of important photographers and imprinted or written names indicating celebrities or notables. Unlike the carte de visite, cabinet cards in albums are normally not a good bargain since the larger size means fewer cards for your money.

Examples of recent sales:

Bundled stack of 50 mixed portrait cabinet cards, antique shop, $25 (50 cents each)

Portrait of a lady wearing large hat and gaudy jewelry, antique shop, $3

Portrait of three well-dressed children, by Lackey, dealer, $3

"Contrived" studio portrait of man in elaborate western costume and "ten-gallon hat," dealer, $5

Fig. 8-9. Oriental Couple by Matthew's Gallery.

Fig. 8-10. Syrian Family by Halladjian.

All early images of ethnic interest are highly sought after by collectors. The first image (Fig. 8-9) is identified on the back: "Sabrico Toyawa, Mutsu Touyawa, Nagasaki, Japan. The second (thankfully) contains the English spelling for the photographer and the town of Ain-Tab.
(Courtesy of the Motzenbecker Collection)

The uncommon cabinet card ($5 to $100)

The *uncommon* cabinet card includes pets, children with toys, people in theatrical costumes, military scenes and portraits, scenics, and art objects. The *uncommon* category also includes portraits by well-known photographers and documentary images. On the upper end of the scale are portraits of celebrities and notables. Also, Spanish-American War images, once all but ignored by collectors, are now coming to the forefront.

Fig. 8-11. Mailman.

(Collection of Gregory Fried)

Fig. 8-12. Boy with Chickens.

As with all 19th century images, anything that makes one cabinet card stand out from the others makes it valuable— whether it be the tools of a person's trade or perhaps his or her hobby. (Courtesy of the Motzenbecker Collection)

Examples of recent sales:

Little girl holding doll, antique shop, $10

Identified family portrait with eight people, by Bascom, dealer, $15

Large cat sleeping on elaborate chair, by Lindsey, antique shop, $20

View of pavilion in the White Mountains, by Kilburn Bros., auction, $25

Stuffed bird on perch in open cage, by Border, dealer, $30

Uniformed Spanish-American War soldier with weapons, by Baker, auction, $40

Well-lit picture of empty chair, by Lloyd, auction, $45

Smiling little girl dressed as "cowgirl," by Norton, antique shop, $45

Group shot of Spanish-American War military company, dealer, $50

Exterior view of bank building and people, including woman holding shotgun, auction, $50

Two Salvation Army women holding tambourines, by Auburn, auction, $50

New York City policeman in uniform with club, by Pleasants, auction, $55

Little girl seated next to scruffy white puppy, by Gleason, auction, $60

Group portrait, city fathers of Nevada City, CA, by Schramm, auction, $65

Fig. 8-13. Group of Miners with Tools.

Images of this type are not only prized by collectors but are of great historical interest due to the highly visible tools. Note the variety of candle holders and oil lamps strapped to their hats. (Courtesy of the Motzenbecker Collection)

Group portrait, three men in miner's clothes, by Stewart, auction, $70

Deceased woman in casket with flowers, by Shinn, auction, $80

View of river docks with identified steamboat, by Nowack, auction, $80

Young boy seated on rocking horse with older sister standing, by Jacobs, auction, $85

Interior scene, Western saloon, auction, $85

Druggist mixing chemicals in front of shelves of medicine, by Hoyt, auction, $90

View of Western ranch, horses in corral, by Arden, dealer, $100

Exterior view of express office in unknown Western town, auction, $100

The rare and premium cabinet card ($100 and up, including albums)

Occasionally, wealthy Victorians put together specialty albums containing extensive collections of cabinet cards by famous travel, art, or celebrity photographers. When found in good condition, these albums can command high prices. Most *rare* cabinet cards are of historical subjects and/or personages–often in series or groupings.

Examples of recent sales:

Portrait of cowboy on white horse, auction, $120

Portrait of Chinese man with young white girl, auction, $135

Six images of Minnesota town after wind storm, by Tenney, auction, $172

Fig. 8-15. Buffalo Bill.

Fig. 8-14. Jack London.

(Courtesy of Swann Galleries, Inc.)

(Collection of Joseph T. Silva)

Not all cabinet cards of celebrities have survived in quantity. The above image of author Jack London in hobo costume is quite rare, as is this particular portrait of Buffalo Bill, which sold at auction in 1998 for $1,150.

Portrait of dog identified as having belonged to President Lincoln, by Pietz, auction, $425

Eight imperial cabinet cards of Yosemite and Colorado scenes, by Hillers, auction, $690

Individual portrait of the Indian chief with ceremonial pipe, by Haynes, auction, $747

Individual portrait of Emperor Norton, whimsical San Francisco character, auction, $1,300

Seven images of Native Americans taken in the 1870s, auction, $1,840

Dating the Cabinet Card

Earliest cabinet card mounts were lightweight and light in color, often with a thin red line near the edge. After 1880, various colors were used, and the area below the image usually contained the photographer's imprint. Cards with gold, beveled edges date from the period 1885 to 1892 (approximately). Maroon-faced cards were produced during the 1880s, and cards from the 1890s often had scalloped or notched edges and were imprinted with elaborate patterns on the back. Because the time periods for these various features often overlapped, cabinet cards are slightly more difficult to date than cartes de visite. Also, many cabinet card photographers used plain, unadorned mounts throughout the period of production.

Although cabinet cards were made by several different processes, most are albumen prints and are subject to fading and foxing; therefore, they should be stored in sleeves or between sheets of acid-free paper, away from light, heat, or moisture.

Fig. 8-16. Prairie Dog Circus?

While it may be difficult to tear your eyes away from the humorous subject of this unusual cabinet card, note the scalloped edges which indicate the image was probably produced in the 1890s. (There are two squirrels in the picture as well.) (Courtesy of the Motzenbecker Collection)

An album of collectible cabinet cards (Courtesy of the Motzenbecker Collection):

Fig. 8-17. Tailor Shop.

Fig. 8-18. Musician.

Fig. 8-19. African-American Family.

Fig. 8-20. Sailboat.

Fig. 8-21. Railroad Workers.

Fig. 8-22. Performing Goats.

Fig. 8-23. Postmortem.

CHAPTER 9

STEREOGRAPHS

ster 'e o graf: A pair of photographs, usually taken with a binocular camera, mounted for three-dimensional viewing in a stereoscope. Concept by Charles Wheatstone; popularized by Sir Charles Brewster (Britain).

Introduced	1851
Peak years	1858-1905
Waned	1910-1925

History of the Stereograph

Stereographs were produced by nearly every photographic process invented during the nineteenth century. (The details of these individual processes are discussed under appropriate chapters.) Stereographs are also referred to as *stereotypes, stereo views, stereoscopic views,* and *stereo cards*. The common use of the term *stereopticon* is incorrect (see Glossary).

the daguerreotype and talbotype. A British physicist, Charles Wheatstone, introduced the concept using binocular engravings. The images were made to combine by the use of mirrors, resulting in a three-dimensional effect. The system was quite impractical, and the discovery went unheralded until the Crystal Palace exhibition of 1851.

The Great Exhibition at the Crystal Palace in London could be described as the first world's fair. The latest inventions, as well as scientific and artistic innovations, were displayed in grand style.

Fig. 9-1. Taxidermic Mountain Goat, stereoscopic daguerreotype.

Stereographic images were produced by every photographic method invented during the 19th century—first as daguerreotypes and calotypes, then as ambrotypes, tintypes, glass slides, albumen prints, and finally as silver prints. Those made by the earliest methods often bring premium prices. (Courtesy of Charles Schwartz, Ltd.)

Although cartes de visite and cabinet cards were produced to some degree as amusements, the primary use of these card formats was portraiture. Stereographs, on the other hand, were produced solely for entertainment and informational purposes (the few individually produced existing stereo portraits are rare exceptions). Today the stereograph is recognized as an excellent source for firsthand information about the people, places, and events of the nineteenth century.

The principle of the stereoscope was actually arrived at one year before the announcements of

Among the various instruments on exhibit was a stereoscope, invented by Sir Charles Brewster, containing binocular daguerreotypes taken with a twin-lens camera. Brewster's binocular camera had been described in the *Journal of the Franklin Institute* in 1849, but it was the exhibition which introduced stereo photography to the world.

Many early stereo images were made either by moving the camera to produce two plates exposed from different angles or by taking separate exposures on two cameras sitting side by side. In 1855, American John Mascher discovered a method for producing two images on one plate

Fig. 9-2. Architectural view, French tissue stereograph.

The commonly applied term "French tissue" is perhaps a bit misleading. The images were produced on albumen or salted paper which was painted on the back with appropriate colors. This image was then sandwiched with a tissue backing into a cardboard frame. The tissue covering made the colored back less obvious, and provided diffusion when the stereograph was viewed by transmitted light. This view was obviously taken for its exaggerated 3-D effect. (Collection of the author)

through the use of "pinhole" photography (see Glossary). Unfortunately, the images were reversed and had to be cut apart for insertion in a viewer.

Mascher's viewer, introduced in 1852, used the design of the basic wood-frame daguerreotype case. He replaced the inside cover pad with a hinged, fold-out leaf containing two magnifying lenses through which the image was viewed. This design was infinitely more convenient than Brewster's viewer of 1851, which was actually an enclosed box with lenses at the top and the daguerreotypes mounted inside on the bottom.

Around 1854, the Langenheim brothers of Philadelphia began one of the first commercial stereograph businesses, selling views of Niagara Falls produced on paper and on positive glass transparencies, which they called "hyalotypes." That same year, the London Stereoscopic Company was started by George Swann Nottage. By 1858, the company had a stockpile of more than 100,000 different stereo images printed on albumen paper from wet-plate negatives. Two other British firms, Gladwells and Negretti & Zambra, also produced large numbers of commercial stereo views during the late 1850s.

In France, several firms were making "tissue" stereographs that could, like a transparency, be viewed by transmitted light. (See color section.) This type of stereograph was also produced in England and America on a lesser scale. While they were most popular during the late 1850s and early 1860s, tissue stereographs were produced throughout the nineteenth century on a limited basis.

By 1860, the advent of the wet plate-albumen print process had revolutionized photography and millions of albumen stereo views were in homes around the world. Large production firms in England, France, and America were manufacturing thousands of stereocards per day. The E. and H. T. Anthony and Company imported large stocks of stereographs and purchased original negatives directly from professional and amateur photographers to be printed and mounted in the company's own production facilities

Fig. 9-3. Fig. 9-4. Mary Queen of Scots, a Prisoner, by J. Elliott, London Stereograph Co., collotype stereograph.

This "series" stereograph was produced by an early printing process that used gelatin-on-glass printing-plates. Not to be confused with the calotype, collotype printing was used throughout the 19th century to produce both black and white and color prints. The example shown contains the blindstamp of the London Stereograph Company. (Collection of the author)

Fig. 9-5. The Wedding, photomechanical copy stereograph.

As with commercially mass-produced card photographs, stereographs were copied freely by anyone who wanted to reproduce them. The popular series, "The Wedding," was copied by several dozen companies. The example shown here is of the lowest quality and likely a copy of a copy. (Collection of the author.)

One of the early promoters of the stereograph was American physician and author Oliver Wendell Holmes, who, along with his friend Joseph Bates, designed what would become the most popular style of stereo viewer. The Holmes-Bates stereoscope incorporated a movable card holder and shielded lenses, and because it was never patented, it was produced by numerous manufacturers until well after the turn of the century.

In the late 1860s, manufacturers began selling mass-produced "series" stereographs. A series was a complete set or several sets of related stereo cards with a single theme or subject. The firms of Charles Pollack (Boston), B.W. Kilburn (New Hampshire), Underwood & Underwood (Kansas), and Keystone View (Pennsylvania) were the major producers of series stereographs from 1870 until World War I.

Series themes are too varied and numerous to allow for an exhaustive list here, but the following are a few examples of series titles: "Niagara Falls"; "The White Mountains of New Hampshire"; "Great Cities"; "California and the West"; "Crystal Palace"; "Churches and Cathedrals"; "Egypt and the Middle East"; "American Civil War"; "Johnstown Flood"; "Chicago Fire"; "Indians"; "Slavery"; "Famous Paintings"; "Sculpture"; and "Tools."

In addition, there were numerous staged series in which actor/models posed for "genre" photographs depicting romantic, dramatic, or comedic stories. Titles representative of this style include "Little Red Riding Hood" (1858), "Gems of American Life" (1871), "The Night Before Christmas" (1870), "Young Ideas" (1870), "Hansel and Gretel" (1872), "The Wedding" (1897), and "The New French Cook" (1900).

The stereograph has been described as "Victorian television." While that is a considerable exaggeration, there are many similarities. Almost every middle- and upper-class home had one or more stereoscopes and many stereoscopic cards. Children fought over who got to look first and which series would be viewed.

Fig. 9-6. Open Blouse, ambrotype stereograph.

Stereoscopic nudes were quite common and popular in France, were they were produced in daguerreotype and ambrotype format, and later by wet-plate process. For obvious reasons, many did not survive into the 20th century, making them highly sought after and highly valuable. (Courtesy of Charles Schwartz, Ltd.)

Fig. 9-7. Street Scene, albumen stereograph.

Larger format stereographs such as this one were often taken by local photographers who then pawned them off on merchants or home owners. In this example, it is unclear whether the subject is the large building, the commercial wagon, or Sharp's Cheap Cash Grocery on the corner. (Courtesy of the Motzenbecker Collection)

The stereograph was at times a form of entertainment for family and friends, and at other times a quiet and private way to escape to some foreign and mysterious land.

A history or geography book could, without difficulty, be illustrated exclusively with stereographs. And, because they were made using every popular form of photography from 1850 to 1925, they provide in themselves a complete history of photography.

The Stereograph Process

Between 1850 and 1925, 10 different types of photographs were used to produce stereographs. Stereo daguerreotypes and calotypes were commonly made by placing two separately exposed images side by side in the viewer; however, a few single-plate stereographs were made in these media during the mid-1850s using "binocular" cameras. Stereo daguerreotypes and

ambrotypes were usually novelty portraits or still lifes, contained in Mascher or Kilburn folding stereo cases or mounted under glass.

Tissue stereographs were simply a type of paper transparency. The image, usually albumen or a salt print, was printed on thin paper, then colors were added (often crudely) to the back of the print. The back was then covered with a piece of tissue to hide the coloring and help diffuse the light, after which the finished product was sandwiched in a cardboard frame. Tiny slits and/or pinholes were sometimes punched through the print to represent points of light or reflections. When viewed by transmitted light, this three-dimensional colored image could present a stunning effect. (See color section.)

During the nineteenth century, more stereographs were produced by the wet plate-albumen print process than by any other method. Stereograph manufacturers sent teams of wet-plate photographers to locations around the world. In addition, original negatives were purchased from freelance professionals and amateurs. Large factories were erected, employing hundreds of workers to print, mount, sell, and ship albumen stereographs. Massive sun-printing frames were built to handle the huge volume of print work. Thousands of stereographs were produced each day, often in addition to an equal volume of cartes de visite and/or cabinet cards. During the peak years, stereographs were available from most major department stores and mail-order houses, as well as from door-to-door salesmen.

Several photomechanical processes were also used to produce stereographs from the early years through the twentieth century. The least common of these were xylographs (from wood engravings) produced during the late 1850s. Another early photomechanical method was the *collotype* (not to be confused with calotype), which was used to produce stereographs from the 1850s until the turn of the century. In the collotype process, the original negative was attached to a glass plate containing a film of dried bi-chromated gelatin and then exposed to bright light. The gelatin hardened in proportion to the amount of light received. When used as a printing plate, the areas of gelatin which were less hardened (highlights) held less ink than the hardened (shadow) areas. Well-made collotypes are sometimes difficult to distinguish from photographs unless they are viewed under magnification.

Half-tone printing (screen printing) is usually thought of as a twentieth-century process; however, stereographs were printed by this method during the 1890s, and some were even printed in color. Before that time, stereographs were hand-tinted, although color collotypes were produced with dubious results. Some hand-tinted stereos are startlingly realistic.

Other stereograph variants included glass positives, cyanotypes, and porcelain prints.

Collecting the Stereograph

Because the stereograph was produced over 75 years of the nineteenth and twentieth centuries, and because of the thousands of theme series that were produced, this format offers more variety for the collector than any other.

Fig. 9-8. "I'm ready when you are," by H. C. White, silver print stereograph.

The heavy dark gray and highly curved mount is indicative of quality mass-produced "real-photo" stereographs of the early 20th century. By this time, cheaper stereographs were being produced by photomechanical printing processes. (Courtesy of the Motzenbecker Collection)

Nearly every imaginable subject was covered by the stereograph at one time or another. Those collectors interested in travel photography will find endless supplies. While there *are* a few rarities among albumen stereos, premium prices are usually reserved for those produced by early, one-of-a-kind processes (daguerreotype, ambrotype, tintype).

What to look for

Early stereographs are usually quite valuable and, fortunately, are easy to identify. While stereo images on glass or metal are almost never found outside of dealers and auction houses, calotype stereographs are occasionally discovered hidden among common cards. Stereographs from the 1850s were mounted in paper frames or, more commonly, on thin cardboard mounts with square corners.

Condition is an important factor in stereo card values. Even in the *common* category, pre-1880 cards in near-mint condition command higher prices. Unless the image is unusual, a stereograph with stains, creases, dog-eared corners, or folds is essentially worthless as a collectible.

Availability/Value Classifications

The common stereograph ($1 to $25)

Approximately 75% of all stereographs on the market are *common*. These are primarily travel images and images from narrative or genre series. Many are mass-produced cards dating from the 1880s and later. A patient collector can often accumulate complete series at a very low cost by diligently searching through the stacks of stereo cards always found at flea markets and in antique shops. The collector should be aware, however, that common stereographs worth no more than $1 or $2 are often overpriced by antique dealers.

Stereo cards with original photographic prints attached are almost always more valuable than printed cards. Those containing albumen prints in mint or near-mint condition are also more valuable.

Among the most interesting *common* stereographs are those made by amateurs just prior to the turn of the century. Well-made amateur stereos of unusual subjects are valuable because they are in most cases one-of-a-kind images.

Fig. 9-9. *"Cedar swamp and turtles," by H. C. White, silver print stereograph.*

(Courtesy of the Motzenbecker Collection)

Fig. 9-10. Art allegory, unknown process.

What is valuable in stereographs is often determined by what interests the collector, and in no area of collectible photography is there more to choose from. (Collection of Gregory Fried)

Examples of recent sales*:

Comic stereo of two well-dressed ladies viewing Hamlet from balcony, antique shop, $3

Amateur stereo of funeral procession, dealer, $5

Turn-of-the-century view of Blacks picking cotton, dealer, $10

Eight cards from the series "The Wedding" published by White, antique shop, $20 lot

Twelve views of European architecture annotated in period hand, antique shop, $25 lot

*Prices are for real-photo stereographs. Mechanically printed stereographs have minimal value.

The uncommon stereograph ($25 to $250)

Most stereo cards in this category date from 1850 to 1880 and account for approximately 25% of the available base. These include views from the American Civil War and documentary images of early disasters, famous expeditions to the Middle East, Africa, and the American West, policemen, firemen, animals, blacks, Indians, sports, and transportation. Early calotype and tissue stereographs are also in this category.

Examples of recent sales*:

Pile of skulls and bones from Spanish cemetery, auction, $35

Teddy Roosevelt on horseback with rifle, auction, $40

Panorama view of San Francisco, marked Warkins' Pacific Coast, auction, $40

Ten views from the series "Ice Storm," Springfield, IL, by Parker, dealer, $50 lot

Overview of Klondike City, Alaska, and Klondike River, by Davis, auction, $55

Interior view of the steamboat Adirondack, by Labarre, auction, $80

"Old Abe" the Wisconsin war eagle sitting on cannon barrel, auction, $100

Fig. 9-12. Eagle Rock by Edward Muybridge, albumen stereograph.

Western scenes by Muybridge are in high demand and are usually priced accordingly. (Courtesy of the Motzenbecker Collection)

Fig. 9-11. San Antonio, Texas by F. Hardesty, albumen stereograph.

Early views of Western towns are highly sought after by collectors. This example is of the highest quality, both from the standpoint of the photography, and the condition of the piece. (Collection of John McWilliams)

Mining prospectors with their pack mules, by Buehman, auction, $125

Complete boxed set of 18 cards titled "The Grande Canyon," antique shop, $150 lot

Portrait stereo of a family of Paiute Indians, by Carter, auction, $175

Eight early French tissue stereos of European architecture, antique shop, $200 lot

The rare stereograph ($250 to $1,000, including sets)

Many of the individual items listed above as *uncommon* could be categorized as *rare* when contained in partial or complete series.

Very early stereographs (1850 to 1855) are *rare*. Daguerreotype and ambrotype stereographs are usually portraiture, still lifes, or art studies (nudes). Interestingly, the tintype is one of the rarest of early stereo formats, primarily due to the domination of other, more suitable media during that period.

Historical images, as well as hard to find "subject" stereos, are in high demand by collectors interested in the "Old West," trains, ships, animals, nudes, etc. Accordingly, they may bring high prices at auction.

Examples of recent sales*:

View of the Navy flagship Lancaster at anchor, by Lawrence & Houseworth, auction, $350

Twenty-five views documenting surveys of the American West, auction, $690 lot

Outdoor portrait of Sioux Chief Shanka Hoska and scout with weapons, auction, $730

Fig. 9-13. Self-portrait by William Henry Jackson, albumen stereograph.

Jackson images in all forms are highly sought after. This stereograph sold at auction in 1998 for $575. (Courtesy of Swann Galleries, Inc.)

Fig. 9-14. Boy on Donkey, ambrotype stereo.

All "hard-image" stereographs bring high prices at sale or auction. This one sold at auction in 1998 for $1,035. (Courtesy of Swann Galleries, Inc.)

Fig. 9-15. Jesse James Postmortem by A. A. Hughes & Brother, albumen stereograph.

This rare stereographic view of the famous bandit in his coffin sold at auction in 1998 for $5,060. (Courtesy of Swann Galleries, Inc.)

The premium stereograph ($1,000 and up, including sets)

Many daguerreotype and other hard imaged stereographs have moved into the premium category in recent years. Also, many views of historic events or portraits of historic personages are in this category, especially when presented in sets or groups.

Examples of recent sales*:

130 views of the Middle and Near East with hand annotations, auction, $1,150 lot

Twenty-nine views of American Indians 1860s-80s, auction, $3,910 lot

Twenty-two views documenting construction of Central Pacific R.R., by Hart, auction, $5,520 lot

Nineteen views documenting George A. Custer's military career, auction, $10,925 lot

Investment Potential

Nearly all stereographs in the *uncommon* and *rare* categories have more than doubled in value during the past decade. Because there are more stereograph collectors today than ever before, even basic "collectibles" are becoming harder to find. In recent years, many stereo images have found their way out of the antique/collectible market and into rare photography sales.

Dating Stereo Cards

Daguerreotype, ambrotype, tintype, and calotype images date from the period of their popularity, mostly before 1860 (see specific chapters on these processes for details). Glass transparencies date from 1850 to 1875. Most mechanically reproduced stereographs (which have the image imprinted directly on the card-mount surface) date from after 1875, although collotypes were made in limited quantities beginning in 1853. Collotype stereos are usually hand-tinted and present a very coarse image.

Although tissue stereographs, mounted in cardboard "frames," were produced from 1857 to 1880, the greater portion date from the period 1865 to 1875.

Albumen stereographs, which make up the bulk of collectible stereo images, were produced from the mid-1850s until around 1900. They are dated by changes in mount shapes and colors. As previously mentioned, earliest cards were lightweight, square, and flat. Colors were pale gray, cream, and white. Starting in the 1860s, a heavier cardboard was used and corners were rounded. Yellow was the most popular color, pale at first, then becoming brighter in the 1870s. A variety of other colors was also used during this period, including a popular orange.

Stereo cards from the 1870s are difficult to date, since this was a transitional period, with a variety of colored mounts holding albumen originals, copy prints, and photomechanical reproductions. In the late 1870s, mount cards were warped (given a lengthwise curve) to increase the illusion of depth and to improve stability. This warped mount became the standard for all stereograph cards manufactured after 1880.

Many stereographs produced after 1890 were lithographic prints, some in color. Some manufacturers continued to use mounted prints, now mostly on silver-bromide paper, exhibiting rich blacks and fine gray tones. These were usually mounted to heavy, warped, dark gray or black mounts.

The stereograph has provided entertainment and information to nearly 150 years of collectors and devotees. In the next decade, it will also bring substantial financial gains to those who have made a wise investment in this most diverse of image collecting fields.

Fig. 9-16. "The bitter end," by G. W. Edmondson, albumen stereograph.

Fig. 9-17. Gathering Hops, albumen stereograph.

The mounts of these two collectible stereographs (one yellow, one orange) are flat with rounded corners, indicating they were produced after 1860 and before the mid-1870s. (Courtesy of the Motzenbecker Collection)

Fig. 9-18. Walking Dudley, a Keystone view, albumen stereograph.

The Keystone View Company was among the most prolific of commercial stereograph producers, operating successfully well into the 20th century. This example was produced in 1893. Note the highly curved mount.
(Courtesy of the Motzenbecker Collection)

Fig. 9-19. Reclining Performer, albumen stereograph.

(Courtesy of the Motzenbecker Collection)

Fig. 9-20. The Ghost, albumen stereograph.

(Courtesy of the Motzenbecker Collection)

Fig. 9-21. Gathering maple syrup, albumen stereograph.

(Courtesy of the Motzenbecker Collection)

Fig. 9-22. *"Our artist at the Falls, Mo. Riv." by F. Jay Haynes, albumen stereograph.*

Haynes was the official photographer for the Northern Pacific Railway. Self-portraits of photographers are highly sought after by collectors. (Courtesy of Charles Schwartz, Ltd.)

CHAPTER 10
LATE NINETEENTH CENTURY PROCESSES

Guide to Identifying Late Nineteenth-Century Print Processes

Early silver bromide or chloride prints, are subject to fading and "silvering"–that is, the silver appears to have surfaced, usually near the edges, exhibiting a metallic sheen. These prints do not ordinarily display the tonal range of carbon or platinum prints.

At first glance, some carbon prints can look very much like well-made bromide prints, except that they do not exhibit the same symptoms of deterioration. When a carbon print is held at a certain angle to the light, the shadows of the image should appear shinier than the highlights and should appear to lie on the surface of the paper, not in it.

Platinum prints exhibit a richness and broad tonal quality unequaled in other processes. Blacks are usually cold black, and grays are silvery (although some brown-toned prints were produced). The surface of the paper has a matte finish, and, under magnification, the image can be seen to be imbedded in the fibers.

History of the Dry Plate, Silver Prints, and Other Late-Nineteenth-Century Printing Process Developments

Despite the overall popularity and the extensive use of the collodion wet-plate process, photographers never ceased complaining about the inconvenience of this messy process. Plate holders and cameras frequently gummed up with sticky collodion residue, and hands were constantly stained from contact with silver nitrate. Traveling photographers had to carry mounds of chemicals and equipment and then, upon locating a prospective scene, quickly unload and set up the portable darkroom so that a plate could be sensitized.

Numerous experiments aimed at producing a dry-plate process were attempted throughout the 1860s and 1870s. British physician Richard

Maddo conceived the idea of gelatin-based photographic plates in 1871, but it was not until improvements were made by Maddox in 1873, and Charles Harper Bennett in 1878, that commercial dry-plate production could become a reality. By 1880, several British manufacturers were producing factory-sensitized, relatively high-speed, ready-to-use photographic plates in quantity. However, photographers were slow to convert to the new plates, mostly because of poor first trials and rumors of inconsistent results.

In the winter of 1880, several tests of the new dry plate were performed by members of the Photographic Association of America, whose report was published in January of 1881. The committee announced that for quality and ease of use, the dry plate was superior in every way to the old wet-plate system of photography.

Still, the high cost of this new plate kept it from achieving overnight success. Each plate had to be purchased from the manufacturer, while with the wet-plate system the glass could be cleaned and reused. It must be remembered that the wet-plate process had been in extensive use longer than any other photographic media to that day. Early trials by photographers well-entrenched in the old system were wrought with costly and discouraging failures.

For the amateur, however, the dry plate was a godsend. Early manufacturers aimed their promotions toward the nonprofessional and even began producing easy-to-use hand-held cameras.

One of these amateurs, working as a bank clerk in Rochester, New York, became interested in dry-plate production, and in 1880 he withdrew his life savings to begin manufacturing plates for E. and H. T. Anthony and Co. Despite early setbacks, the young man turned his small manufacturing business into a photographic empire which today is the largest and most recognized supplier of image-making materials in the world. The man's name was George Eastman.

Eastman's competitors during those early years were John Carbutt (Keystone Plates), Cramer and Norden of St. Louis, and Edward Anthony (Defiance Plates). Despite this stiff competition, Eastman was able to hold his own in the dry-plate business, while at the same time developing gelatin roll film (1884) and the Kodak detective camera

Fig. 10-1. Spanish American War Officers, silver print.

Less than a decade ago, images of the Spanish American War could be found at flea markets and on dealer tables for only a few dollars. While group shots such as this one have always been highly collectible, this area of collecting has come into its own in recent years and values are steadily rising. This print sold at auction in 1998 for $1,265. (Courtesy of Swann Galleries, Inc.)

(1888). The name *Kodak* was conceived by Eastman simply because it was easy to pronounce and remember. So many varieties of Kodak cameras were produced during the early years that several guidebooks have been published covering just this one brand of camera.

In 1880, while the Photographic Association was testing dry plates, a British firm was introducing a new type of printing paper with a similar gelatin-based emulsion. Called bromide (or silver-bromide) paper, it surpassed albumen paper in both speed and convenience. Like the dry plate, bromide paper achieved early success in England, but it was not well known in America until 1887, when a court battle erupted between former associates George Eastman and Edward Anthony. Suits were brought by both sides for infringement of patent rights relating to the manufacture of the new gelatin-based paper. An out-of-court settlement was made which allowed both sides to continue production.

There were many problems with stability and quality control in the early gelatin-silver papers (the faded condition of many extant bromide prints bears witness to this). By the turn of the century, many professionals were using the more permanent and more expensive Velox (see, below) and carbon prints for their important work, leaving bromide paper for "cheap" prints. Many photographers still considered albumen paper superior, but nevertheless opted for the convenience of bromide.

Fig. 10-2. Opium Den Paraphernalia by Larson, silver print.

Early images taken anywhere in the western U.S. have always been considered "Old West" images, even if they were taken around the turn of the century. This photograph of law enforcement officials posing with the "take" from a raid on Goldfield Nevada's Dream Land opium den has that appeal and more. (Collection of Joseph T. Silva)

Velox or silver-chloride prints

Velox was a gelatin-chloride paper which came on the market around 1893. Some photographers (especially amateurs) preferred it because it was less sensitive than bromide papers and could be handled in dim light. Bromide papers required complete darkness or special safelights. Because they were printed by artificial light sources, Velox and other chloride papers were given the nickname "gaslight paper."

Carbon prints

The basic concept of the carbon print had been around since the 1830s and was patented by Frenchman Alphonse Poitevin in 1855.

However, the process produced poor tonal gradation, a failing remedied by Joseph Swan in his modified carbon process of 1866. Eventually capable of superb tonal range and extreme permanence, carbon prints were popular for exhibition images by art photographers at the turn of the century.

Platinum print

The platinum print process was also experimented with during the early years of photography, but it did not achieve notoriety until a paper was published by two Austrian photographers in 1882. Relying on elaborate chemical reactions, the process produced an image consisting of pure platinum. Prints produced by this process exhibit superior tonal qualities and are extremely stable and permanent.

The innovations discussed here were forerunners of the modern photographic process, and, in fact, some of these methods are still in use for exhibition printing. The top photographic suppliers of the era, such as Anthony and Scovills (later Ansco) and Eastman Kodak, helped make photography an essential element of twentieth-century life.

The Dry-Plate, Silver-Print Process

At the turn of the century, photographers had their choice of three types of cameras: one which used dry plates, one which used roll film, or one which used both. Because roll film did not come into extensive use until after the turn of the century, we concern ourselves here with dry-plate photography as practiced beginning in the late 1880s.

Fig. 10-3. Chicago World's Fair by C. D. Arnold, platinum print.

This image is one of a pair of platinum prints of the fair that sold at auction in 1998 for $632 the lot. (Courtesy of Swann Galleries, Inc.)

Fig. 10-4. Seed's Dry-plates.

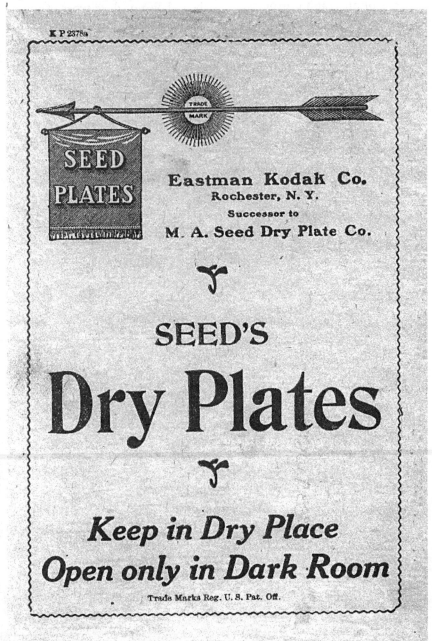

After helping to introduce the dry-plate to photographers in the 1880s, George Eastman became successful enough to buy out many of his competitors, including the M. A. Seed Dry-plate Co. Eastman Kodak continued to market the plates under Seed's familiar name. (Collection of the author)

Dry plates were purchased from a supplier in a light-tight container. In a darkroom, by the dim glow of a safelight called a "ruby lamp," the plates were inserted into plate holders. Because it was difficult to tell which side of the plate was which, the photographer would touch his tongue to an area near the edge, knowing that the film side of the plate would be tacky.

One by one, the film holders were inserted into the camera and the various exposures made. By this time, cameras were equipped with adjustable diaphragms and shutters, allowing easy adjustment for changes in light intensity. When the photographic session was over, the holders containing exposed plates were carried back to the darkroom for developing.

A number of developing solutions were used during the early years. Ferrous oxalate and pyrogallic acid ("pyro") were among the first. Amateurs, who in their enthusiasm produced large quantities of images, complained about developer stains and the constant changing of spoiled pyro. This prompted the introduction of other formulas, primarily metol hydrochinon ("metol"), which could be produced from powders as needed. After development, the plate was fixed in hypo, washed, and dried.

Although enlargers were at this time coming into use, contact printing was still the common method. Two different types of paper could be used: developing paper (bromide or chloride) or printing-out paper (aristotype, lithium, or albumen). Developing papers (exposed by gaslight) required a developing agent to bring out the latent image, while printing-out papers (exposed in sunlight) darkened with exposure and required toning. The developer for paper was the same metol solution used for plates. Finished prints were fixed, then washed and dried as usual. As part of the mounting process, prints were often burnished–that is, run between hot rollers to induce a hard, glossy finish.

As more and more amateurs became involved in photography, commercial processing plants were opened to save snapshot takers from the mess of developing. One early Kodak film camera came pre-loaded with film. After the roll was exposed, the entire camera was shipped back to Kodak for film development, mounting, and reloading. As the new century approached, photography appeared to have reached the ultimate in convenience.

Collecting Silver and Platinum Prints

While bromide- and chloride-based gelatin prints were produced in quantity by amateurs and professionals, "permanent" print processes, such as carbon and platinum, were used primarily by professionals for works which they considered important. Therefore, with noted exceptions, most bromide- or chloride-based prints are considered *common*, while most carbon or platinum prints can be classified as *uncommon* or *rare*.

Availability/Value Classifications

Common late 19th century prints ($1 to $10)

Bromide and chloride prints, produced in quantity by amateurs and professionals, encompass a variety of subjects and scenes. All good-quality silver prints which can be specifically dated to the period 1880 to 1900 are valuable as being representative of the early years of the process. Some beautifully artistic images, produced by "unknown" photographers, are available for very low prices. While they will probably never command high prices, these images are now receiving appreciation for their aesthetic and historic merit.

Examples of recent sales:

7" x 9" silver print of little girl with dog in outdoor setting, antique shop, $5

7" x 9" silver print of unknown family in front of house, antique shop, $7

6" x 8" silver print of two young boys on very large mule, antique shop, $10

10" x 12" silver print of well-dressed twelve-member family front of large fireplace, dealer, $10

Fig. 10-5. Two men taking snuff, gum-bichromate print.

Probably English in origin, this gum-bichromate print was likely taken by a supporter of the Photo-Secession movement. Achieved through a complicated process, gum-bichromates often resembled watercolor prints, with soft focus and subtle tints. (Collection of Julie and Dominic Santangelo)

Uncommon late 19th century prints ($10 to $100)

Silver prints of exceptional note and those produced by well-known photographers will bring higher prices. Because of the nature of their use, unattributed carbon and platinum prints are valuable as being representative of the processes. When identified, even those by lesser known artists can bring high prices.

Examples of recent sales:

3" circular Kodak silver print of four men on steps of house, dealer, $12

7" x 9" silver print of street scene, unknown western town, dealer, $25

6" x 8" silver print of unknown actress in risqué costume, $25

10" x 12" silver print of man wearing badge sitting in front of South Dakota home, auction, $30

7" x 9" silver print of farrier shoeing a horse, antique shop, $35

8" x 10" silver print of butcher standing in front of his shop, meat in window, dealer, $50

8" x 9" platinum print of five women each dressed in different sports attire, auction, $85

7" x 9" silver print of identified comedian in black-face, auction $90

7" x 9" carbon print of pretty Indian girl in feathered headdress, dealer, $95

Rare late 19th century prints ($100 to $3,000)

Silver and platinum prints of unusual merit and/or attributed to well-known photographers are offered by dealers and auction houses at nearly every photographic sale.

Examples of recent sales:

7" x 9" silver print of unknown western fort seen from a distance, dealer, $125

6" x 8" silver print of Saturday Evening Post delivery boy with bicycle, auction, $130

Group of three 5" x 6" cyanotypes of Idaho scenes, auction, $230

8" x 9" silver print of "bottle player" standing next to rack of bottles, auction, $250

7" x 9" silver print of 1890s baseball team for Pittsburgh academy, auction, $316

16" x 20" silver print of Big Chief Mine, Colorado, by Jackson, auction, $862

11" x 15" silver print of Rodin statuary by Rodin's official photographer Druet, auction, $1,610

18" x 24" silver print of Navajo sheep in Arizona with photographer's signature, auction, $1,955

Fig. 10-6. Big Chief Mine by William Henry Jackson, silver print.

This famed western photographer gradually changed from albumen to silver print processes as new century approached, and no doubt reprinted many of his earlier works as silver prints. This 16" x 20" print sold at auction in 1998 for $862. (Courtesy of Swann Galleries, Inc.)

Premium late 19th century prints ($3,000 and up, including sets and collections)

Examples of recent sales:

Collection of 126 platinum, silver, and other media of India in the 1890s, auction, $4,140

Framed 35" x 49" linen-mounted silver print of President McKinley, by Shaw, auction, $4,600

Collection of 55 cyanotypes (with ephemera) related to the Canadian Railroad, auction, $6,440

Although these processes received more extensive use after 1900, for the collector of nineteenth-century images, they represent the culmination of 60 years of photographic experimentation and progress. Throughout the 1800s, photography had been very much a personal experience for those involved. The elaborate processes required individual patience and diligence to achieve any sort of quality in the finished image. There were amateurs, but even they had to be dedicated to the art, for those who were not quickly gave up in frustration.

With the advent of hand-held cameras, dry plates, roll film, and presensitized paper, photography became easy. Anyone who could aim a lens and push a button could take a picture. This meant that those who called themselves "photographers" now had to prove their worth. The degree of their success is reflected today in the value we have placed on their works.

Fig. 10-7. Josephine Marcus Earp?, silver print.

A rare and surprising photograph of a woman believed to be Wyatt Earp's wife in diaphanous sheath. Important for its historical value alone, it is as well a quality image of a beautiful subject. The negative was made in the 1880s and printed after the turn of the century. The image sold at auction in 1998 for $4,600. (Courtesy of Swann Galleries, Inc.)

Fig. 10-8. Photograph of the Moon by Lewis Rutherford, woodburytype.

Woodburytypes, made through an early photomechanical printing process, were often "tipped in" to books as illustrations. They generally exhibit rich brown multi-dimensional tones. This one sold at auction in 1998 for $1,495. (Courtesy of Swann Galleries, Inc.)

Fig. 10-9. Chief Joseph of the Nez Pierce by Everett G. Cummings, printing out paper.

This rare and important image of Native Americans on horseback was printed on gelatin silver printing-out paper, which slowly began to take the place of albumen paper in the 1890s. (Courtesy of Swann Galleries, Inc.)

Fig. 10-10. Zuni Governor by Edward Curtis, platinum print.

Even in reproduction, the fine texture and tonal quality of the platinum process can be seen in this magnificent portrait taken around the turn of the century. (Courtesy of Etherton Gallery)

Fig. 10-11. Qahatika Girl by Edward Curtis, photogravure.

Produced through a superior photomechanical printing process, photogravure prints provided near-photo quality images for limited runs to be sold or used as illustrations in books. (Courtesy of Etherton Gallery)

CHAPTER 11
AMERICAN CIVIL WAR IMAGES

American Civil War images were produced by ambrotype, tintype, carte de visite, and albumen print processes. War-related images were made as early as 1858, and as late as 1870, even though the war itself lasted from 1861 to 1865.

Collecting American Civil War Images

A unique area of photograph collecting involves images produced in America during the period of the American Civil War. Although hundreds of thousands of images relating to the conflict were produced, demand from museums, historians, and collectors makes them relatively scarce and comparatively expensive.

Fig. 11-1. Earl Van Dorn, C.S.A., carte de visite.

(Collection of the author.)

Of the various formats which make up the collectible base for this field, the largest percentage are cartes de visite (50%), followed by tintypes (25%), stereographs (15%), ambrotypes (10%), and large albumen prints and daguerreotypes (less than 1%). The values of Civil War images reflect this relative availability–cartes are the easiest to locate and the least expensive, while war-related daguerreotypes and albumen prints

are seldom found outside of dealer and auction houses, where they are in great demand.

Tintypes are found both in carte de visite-sized mounts and cased in the style of daguerreotypes. Collectors are cautioned that tintypes are often not original to their cases, having been placed there to improve their appearance and value. Original-case tintypes command higher prices than loose or sleeved examples, especially if case elements indicate that the image was made early in the war.

Fig. 11-2. Black soldier, carte de visite-sized tintype in brass frame.

(Collection of Gregory Fried)

Ambrotypes were produced less frequently as the war progressed, and therefore most existing ambrotype images are from the early part of the war. Special attention should be given to ambrotypes of officers, since most soldiers who achieved rank early were rapidly promoted and, if they survived, may have become important high-ranking officers by the war's end.

Fig. 11-3. Unknown soldier, 1/4-plate milk glass print.

(Collection of Richard and Gloria Schroeder)

Cartes de visite of individual soldiers were produced in large quantities when new recruits heading for battle lined up to have portraits made in their new uniforms. As troops on the march passed through various towns along the way, soldiers would often head for the nearest photographic establishment, eager to show off a scruffy new beard or well-earned gold stripes. Thousands of images were sent by mail in both directions. Often the photographer would include mailing services in the cost of the portrait.

As the war progressed, manufacturers of mass-produced cartes and stereographs began to take advantage of the excellent images being produced by Brady, O'Sullivan, Gardner, and other battlefield photographers. Primary among distributors of war-related images was E. and H. T. Anthony and Co., which marketed battle and encampment scenes, as well as portraits of military heroes, until well after the end of the war. The collector should be aware that stereographs

produced long after the war ended are far less valuable. Also, while cartes de visite do exist with actual autographs on them, thousands of cartes of famous Civil War personages were mass-produced with printed signatures.

Fig. 11-4. Unknown soldier, in "sweetheart" case.

(Collection of Richard and Gloria Schroeder)

Availability/Value Classifications

The common Civil War image ($20 to $100)

"Common" is perhaps misleading in this field as all Civil War images are highly sought after. The "lower-priced" category consists entirely of cartes de visite and sleeved or loose tintype portraits and makes up approximately 60% of the collectible base. These are occasionally available at flea markets and antique shops, or they can be purchased from photographica and military artifact dealers. Prices of common Civil War images have increased nearly tenfold in the past decade. Carte de visite portraits of soldiers are sometimes found in albums or stacks of cards that have not yet been thoroughly scrutinized by collectors. Civil War uniforms were varied and are not always easily recognizable as being of military origin (especially uniforms of the Confederacy). Seasoned collectors learn to recognize the "look" of a military image.

Fig. 11-5. Union Zouave, carte de visite.

(Collection of Jerry Mack)

Loose tintype of unidentified soldier, patriotic backdrop, $65

CDV, General George McClellan and wife, auction, $70

1/9 plate tintype bust shot of unidentified soldier, antique shop, $75

CDV, unidentified officer with sword, auction, $85

CDV, unidentified soldier with butts of pistols showing on each side, auction, $95

1/6 plate tintype three-quarter pose of unidentified soldier, dealer, $100

Fig. 11-6. Confederate Cavalryman, 1/6-plate tintype.

(Collection of Joseph T. Silva)

Examples of recent sales:

CDV, identified Union soldier, antique shop, $25

CDV, unidentified Union soldier, standing pose, dealer, $35

Tinted gem tintype in CDV sleeve, Union artillery sergeant, antique shop, $35

CDV, identified soldier by Miller of Vermont, auction, $50

CDV, identified soldier by Morse & Peaslee of Nashville, auction, $50

The uncommon Civil War image ($100 to $500)

Primary to this category are cased images, identified portraits of officers, portraits containing weapons and accouterments, and "production" cartes and stereographs. Specific prices are based primarily on the changing factors of supply and demand of the particular type of image in question. About 20% of existing Civil War images can be considered *uncommon*.

Fig. 11-7. "Intelligent Contrabands at leisure," by Alexander Gardner, albumen stereograph.

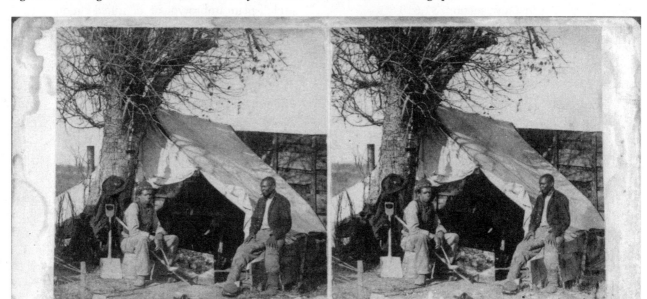

One of group of six Civil War stereographs that sold at auction in 1998 for $1,150 the lot. (Courtesy of Swan Galleries, Inc.)

Examples of recent sales:

CDV, hand tinted of California soldier by Cook of San Francisco, auction, $110

CDV, showing nine Confederate generals in individual vignettes, auction, $125

1/6 plate tintype of young soldier holding rifle, antique shop, $150

CDV, Confederate General Pike by Anthony, auction, $165

CDV, two soldiers, one on crutches with right leg amputated, auction, $181

CDV, Confederate General Hanson in Napoleonic pose, auction, $190

1/4 plate tintype of soldier with weapons, patriotic backdrop, dealer, $200

"Pocketbook" CDV album containing 10 images of various soldiers, dealer, $300

CDV, identified person carrying "Sanitary Flour" with U.S. flags, auction, $350

Group of three CDVs of General Sherman, auction, $402

The rare Civil War image ($500 to $2,500)

This category represents one of the strongest areas of photographic investment. Offerings at auctions often surpass their high estimates, and some bring two and three times the expected price. Primary in this category are images by well-known photographers and portraits of important military figures. Albums and collections may also fall into this price category.

Examples of recent sales:

Two 1/6 plate ambrotypes of unidentified soldiers in side-by-side Union case, dealer, $550

9" x 11" albumen view of 43rd Mass Infantry at Camp Rogers, NC, auction, $632

8" x 12" albumen view of Orange & Essex RR depot by Russell, auction, $920

6" x 8" albumen print of soldiers at leisure from Gardner's "Sketchbook," auction, $1,092

1/4 plate of young black cavalry sergeant with sword wearing gauntlets, auction, $1,500

Half plate of four soldiers in kepis standing in a row, auction, $1,610

Half plate of soldier in front of elaborate regimental backdrop, auction, $1,610

Album of 45 CDVs and tintypes of various soldiers, auction, $1,840

Album of 15 CDVs of Confederate officers by Brady and others, auction, $1,840

1/6 plate tintypes, one of CW drummer and one of CW fifer, in Union case, auction, $2,175

1/6 plate ambrotype of identified Confederate private, with bio, auction, $2,300

Examples of some recent sales:

Half-plate ambrotype of identified Union officer, in Union case, dealer, $2,500

Group of ten CDVs of various soldiers including wounded and starved, auction, $2,760

Group of mixed tins and ambrotypes of various soldiers and officers, auction, $3,220

Group of 62 CDV portraits of various soldiers and officers, auction, $3,910

Five unmounted albumen prints of encampments and soldiers, auction, $3,910

Fig. 11-8. General George Armstrong Custer by Mathew Brady, albumen stereograph.

One of a group of 19 Custer-related stereographs that sold at auction in 1998 for $10,925 the lot. (Courtesy of Swan Galleries, Inc.)

The premium Civil War image ($2,500 and up)

High-quality war-related daguerreotypes and ambrotypes, unique albums and collections, and a few very rare individual images are considered to be premium examples Civil War image collecting.

Civil War Revenue Tax Stamps

During the period from August 1864 to August 1866, the U.S. government instituted a law requiring that a tax stamp be attached to the back of specific types of photographs, and that it be canceled by the selling establishment at the time of the sale. The denomination of the stamp was proportionate to the cost of the photograph: 2 cents for images that cost less than 25 cents each; 3 cents for images that cost 25 to 50 cents; 5 cents for images that cost 50 cents to $1; and 5 cents for each additional dollar of cost.

Many types and colors of stamps were used; however, the blue 2-cent "playing cards" stamp is significant because it was used during the summer of 1866. While images with this stamp can be specifically dated to the summer of that year, other stamps can also be significant when the cancellation includes a date. All photographs

with Civil War tax stamps affixed are slightly more valuable because they can be positively dated to that period.

The collector who chooses to specialize in American Civil War images should become familiar with all aspects of that conflict. A knowledge of uniforms, insignias, weapons, and accoutrements is a must. More than a basic knowledge of names and locations is required (military leaders, heroes, battles, and towns). As with all photographs that relate to a specific historical event, Civil War images can only gain in value as time passes. This specialty is both demanding and rewarding.

Fig. 11-9. Fig. 11-10. Lt. D. W. Reed, Company C, 12th Iowa Infantry, carte de visite.

The collector is lucky indeed if he or she acquires an image upon which is found the name and location of the photographer; the name, rank, and regimental information of the sitter, and a tax stamp. (Collection of the author.)

Fig. 11-11. Brothers, 1/6-plate ambrotypes.

It would be easy, and perhaps a bit romantic, to assume that one brother is Union and the other Confederate. Since the younger brother's uniform shows no visible insignia, and since both the Northern and Southern armies wore uniforms in every imaginable color and material, the truth will never be known. (Collection of Kathryn Mace)

APPENDIX A

Nineteenth-Century Photographers of Note

Several million people were involved in the production of photographic images from 1839 to 1900. A large number of these were superb artists whose works have survived to this day, much to the delight of collectors. However, only a handful of these photographers made their mark on photographic history, and these are the names that collectors' dreams are made of. Dates given throughout are "in business" dates for each photographer.

Adamson, Robert. Scotland; 1842-60; calotypes.
Some of the best early photographic work was done by the team of Hill & Adamson, primarily portraiture and architectural views. *Rare* and *premium*.

Alinari, Fratelli. Italy; 1850s to 1880s; albumen prints.
Famous for architectural views of Italian landmarks. *Rare* and *premium* (albums).

Allen, Amos. United States; 1852-93; daguerreotypes, albumen prints, card photographs.
Famous for daguerreotype profile portraits and later for documentation of Pennsylvania mining towns. *Uncommon* and *rare*.

Anderson, James. Italy; 1850s to 1860s; albumen prints.
Produced views of Roman architecture. *Rare*.

Annan, James Craig. Scotland; 1890s; carbon prints.
Son of Thomas Annan, James was also known for his architectural photography. *Rare*.

Annan, Thomas. Scotland; 1868-77; carbon prints.
Famous for his photographs of the streets of Glasgow which were published in volumes around 1878. *Rare*.

Anson, Rufus. United States; 1851-67; daguerreotypes, ambrotypes, card photographs.
Unlike most early photographers, Anson often imprinted his name on his works on the plate and/or mat, making them more valuable to today's collectors. His heavily patronized gallery was in New York City. *Uncommon*.

Anthony, Charles J. United States; 1850s; daguerreotypes.
Inventor of the "magic background" vignetting process, which produced unusual patterns around the image. Unfortunately, his work is rarely identified. *Rare*.

Anthony, Edward. United States; 1850-74; daguerretypes, stereo, albumen, and card photographs.
A prominent figure in American photography, Anthony produced daguerreotypes at a New York gallery until 1847 at which time he started concentrating on manufacture and supply of photographic materials. Daguerreotypes by his hand are rare; cartes de visite and stereos with his imprint are *uncommon*.

Atget, Jean-Eugène-Auguste. France; 1890s; gelatin print.
While primarily a twentieth-century photographer, Atget's early works are especially in demand. Mostly exteriors, statuary, fountains, etc. *Rare*.

Babbitt, Platt D. United States; 1853-70; daguerreotypes, albumen prints.
Operated an outdoor gallery at Niagara, with the falls as backdrop. Daguerreotypes *rare* and *premium*; other work *uncommon*.

Baldus, Edouard-Denis. France; 1850s to 1860s; calotypes, albumen prints, salt prints.
Produced exterior views, fountains, statuary, etc. Early works (calotypes, salt prints) rare and premium; later albumen and reprints *uncommon*.

Ball, James P. United States; 1845-74; daguerreotypes, albumen prints, card photographs.
Well-known early black daguerreotypist practiced in Cincinnati, Ohio. Documented slave trade and plantation life. *Rare*.

Barnard, George. United States; 1850s to 1880s; daguerreotypes, albumen, and card photographs.
Member of "Brady's Photographic Corps" famous for photographing the people and places of the American Civil War. Daguerreotypes *premium*; war-related prints *rare*; others *uncommon*.

Bayard, Hippolyte. France; 1850s; daguerreotypes, calotypes, albumen prints.
One of the early pioneers of photography. *Premium*.

Beard, Richard. England; 1840s to 1850s; daguerreotypes.
One of London's leading early daguerreotypists. *Premium*.

Bedford, Francis. England; 1850s to 1860s; albumen and cartes de visite.
Specialized in cathedrals and British landscapes. *Uncommon*, some *rare*.

Bell, William. United States; 1870s; albumen prints.
One of a group of well-known photographers who documented expansion into the American West. Specialized in expansive views. *Rare*.

Bisson, Auguste-Rosalie and Louis-Auguste. France; 1840s to 1860s; calotypes and salt prints, daguerreotypes, albumen prints.
Known for their spectacular Alpine views, these brothers also photographed cathedrals. *Rare*.

Black, James. United States; 1845-70; daguerreotypes, albumen prints.
Partner in daguerreotype gallery of John Whipple. Took first aerial photographs (wet plate) in 1860. *Rare*.

Blanquart-Evrard, Louis-Désiré. France; 1846-67; calotypes, salt prints, albumen prints.
Introduced the albumen print in 1850. His firm produced a number of illustrated books and mounted images by various photographers in both salt and albumen prints. *Rare* and *premium* (books).

Bogardus, Abraham. United States; 1846-87; daguerreotype, ambrotype, tintype, albumen, cartes de visite, cabinets.

This well-known New York daguerreotypist later became the first president of the National Photographic Association. Cased images *rare*; others *uncommon*.

Bonfils, Felix. France; 1870s; albumen prints.

Made photographic excursions throughout the Middle East from his studio in Lebanon. Work includes views of landmarks and architecture. *Rare*.

Boughton, Alice. United States; 1890s; platinum and gelatin prints.

Primarily a portrait photographer at the turn of the century. Associated with Gertrude Kasebier. *Rare*.

Bourne, Samuel. England; 1860s; albumen prints.

Famous for his views of landmarks and landscapes of India. Produced small-format albumen studies (4"x 8"). *Rare*.

Brady, Mathew. United States; 1843-90; daguerreotypes, ambrotypes, tintypes, albumen prints, cartes de visite, cabinets.

Probably the most recognized name in nineteenth-century American photography. Produced many daguerreotypes of celebrities and politicians of the period. Famous for photographs of the Civil War, although many images which bear his name were not taken by him. Cased images and albumen prints *rare* or *premium*; others *uncommon*.

Braun, Adolphe. France; 1840-70; daguerreotypes, albumen prints, stereographs, and cartes de visite.

Took mountain and landscape views of Switzerland. Famous for instantaneous street scenes (stop-action). *Rare*.

Britt, Peter. United States; 1870s to 1880s; daguerreotypes, albumen prints.

Britt was one of the earliest daguerreotypists to open a studio in the American northwest (Jacksonville, Oregon, 1852). In later years, he helped to document Westward expansion. *Rare*.

Broadbent, Samuel. United States; 1840-80; daguerreotypes, ambrotypes, cartes de visite, cabinets, stereographs.

This accomplished daguerreotypist operated studios in Georgia (1843-47), Delaware (1848-50), and Philadelphia (1851-80). For many of his daguerreotype portraits he used a distinctive painted backdrop. Cased images *rare*; others *uncommon*.

Cameron, Julia Margaret. England; 1860s to 1870s; albumen prints.

One of the most recognized names in late nineteenth-century photography, Cameron produced superb "character" portraits, especially of children. Her images were often softly lit and focused, giving the effect of a Renaissance painting. Even though her prints were commercially produced in some quantity, the high demand from collectors has made them *rare*.

Carjat, Étienne. France; 1855-75; albumen prints, cartes de visite.

Well-known and influential French portraitist, a contemporary of Nadar. Their works, published in Galerie Contermporaine, are sought after by collectors, as are individual cartes de visite. *Uncommon* or *rare*.

Carroll, Lewis. England; 1850s to 1860s; albumen prints, cartes de visite.

The author of Alice in Wonderland also produced some superb artistic photographs, primarily portraits and "staged" scenes. *Rare* or *premium*.

Carvalho, Soloman. United States; 1849-80; daguerreotypes, albumen prints, cartes de visite.

One of the earliest photographers to accompany an expedition to the American West (John C. Fremont expedition, 1853-54). Operated galleries in Baltimore and in New York City. Daguerreotypes and albumen prints *rare*; cartes de visite *uncommon*.

Chase, Lorenzo. United States; 1844-56; daguerreotypes.

Unlike that of most daguerreotypists, Chase's work can often be identified by an imprint in the brass mat, making his work *uncommon* or *rare*.

Claudet, Antoine François Jean. France/England; 1841-54; daguerreotypes, calotypes, albumen prints, cartes, stereographs.

The premier British daguerreotypist. *Rare* and *premium*.

Clifford, Charles. Spain; 1850s; albumen prints.

Produced views of Spanish landscapes and architecture, as well as photographs of armor. *Rare*.

Cook, George Smith. United States; 1840-80; daguerreotypes, ambrotypes, tintypes, cartes de visite, albumen prints.

Very active in daguerreotype, especially in Charleston, South Carolina. One of the best-known Confederate photographers during the Civil War. *Rare*; cartes de visite *uncommon*.

Daguerre, Louis-Jacques-Mandé. France; 1838-51; daguerreotypes.

As the inventor of the process which bore his name, and due to his early death, Daguerre's works are priceless. *Premium*.

Day, Fred Holland. United States; 1880s to 1890s; platinum prints.

Progressive and controversial turn-of-the century photographer famous for his photographic reenactment of the "Passion of Our Lord" (1898). *Rare* or *premium*.

Delamotte, Philip H. Britain; 1840s to 1850s; calotypes.

One of several important amateur calotypists, Delamotte is known for his documentation of the construction of the Crystal Palace. *Rare*.

Demachy, Robert. France; 1880s to 1890s; platinum prints.

This prominent French photographer of the period produced highly artistic images in the style of the Photo-Secession group. *Rare*.

Disdéri, André-Adolphe-Eugène. France; 185489; daguerreotypes, albumen prints, cartes de visite, stereographs.

Known for popularizing the carte de visite. Early images *rare*; later works *uncommon*.

Du Camp, Maxime. France; 1840s to 1850s; calotypes.

One of a group of superb French calotypists whose works often appeared as Blanquart-Evrard plates. Images include Middle-Eastern views. *Rare*.

Eakins, Thomas. United States; 1880s to 1890s; platinum prints.

Produced motion studies, portraits, and nudes in the artistic style of a painter-cum-photographer. *Premium*; some *rare*.

Eastman, Walter. United States; 1848-56; daguerreotypes.

Accomplished daguerreotypist whose name appears as successor on Plumbe gallery advertising cards attached to the backs of certain images. *Uncommon*.

Edwards, Jonas. United States; 1841-46; daguerreotypes.

Partner in the "National Portrait Gallery" with Edward Anthony. *Rare*.

Emerson, Peter Henry. England; 1880s to 1890s; platinum prints.

Vocal supporter of the "naturalist" school in art photography, precursor of the Photo-Secession group. Known for his series Life and Landscape on the Norfolk Broads. *Rare*.

Evans, Frederick. England; 1880s to 1890s; platinum prints.

Another of the pre-Secessionist "art" photographers, Evans specialized in superb architectural views of cathedrals. He also did portraits of art and literary notables. *Rare*.

Fenton, Roger. England; 1850 to 1860s; calotypes, albumen prints, stereographs.

This prolific British photographer, the first to document the hazards and effects of war (Crimea 1855), is also famous for his still-life images. Fenton also produced many excellent travel and architectural views. *Rare* or *premium*.

Fitzgibbon, John. United States; 1846-82; daguerreotypes, ambrotypes, tintypes, cartes de visite, cabinets.

Well-known St. Louis portraitist and early Western itinerant daguerreotypist. Long and successful career produced many excellent images. Early work *rare*; later work *uncommon*.

Fontayne, Charles. United States; 1846-58; daguerreotype.

Specialized in full-plate daguerreotype panoramas and life-size paper photographs. *Rare*.

Fredricks, Charles De Forest. United States; 1852-94; daguerreotypes, ambrotypes, cartes de visite, cabinets.

Eminent New York daguerreotypist who later helped popularize the carte de visite in America. Had branch gallery in Cuba (1850s). Cased images, often identified by imprint on brass mat, *rare*; later images *uncommon*.

Frith, Francis. England; 1850s to 1880s; albumen prints.

Well-known and prolific British photographer produced excellent series of images depicting "Egypt, Sinai, and Jerusalem." Primarily a travel photographer. *Rare* and *premium*; some *uncommon*.

Gardner, Alexander. United States; 1860s to 1880s; albumen prints, cartes de visite, stereographs.

One of the premier photographers of the American Civil War, *Gardner's Photographic Sketch Book of the War* series is prized by collectors (*premium*). Later, Gardner produced images of Westward expansion. Individual Western and war-related images, *rare*; stereos and cartes de visite *rare* and *uncommon*.

Gouraud, Francois. France; 1839-48; daguerreotypes.

Agent for Daguerre, Gouraud produced numerous "sample" images and practiced portraiture at Niagara Falls in 1842. *Premium*.

Griswold, Victor. United States; 1850-72; daguerreotypes, ambrotypes, tintypes.

Best known as the inventor of ferrotype plates, competitor to Neffs melainotype (tintype). *Rare*.

Gurney, Jeremiah. United States; 1840-85; daguerreotypes, ambrotypes, cartes de visite, cabinets, albumen prints.

One of the most active and honored American portrait photographers. *Rare*; some cartes de visite and cabinets *uncommon*.

Haynes, Frank Jay. United States; 1870s to 1890s; albumen prints.

One of a group of photographers documenting Westward expansion. Employed by the Northern Pacific Railroad. *Rare*.

Hesler, Alexander. United States; 1847-90; daguerreotypes, ambrotypes, cartes de visite, cabinets, albumen prints.

Noted American photographer for almost half a century. Hesler's daguerreotype of Minnehaha Falls was the inspiration for Longfellow's epic poem Hiawatha. Pioneered dry-plate photography in the United States. Early work *rare*; cabinets and cartes de visite *uncommon*.

Hill, David Octavius. England; 1840s to 1850s; calotypes.

The team of Hill and Adamson was to British calotype what the Southworth and Hawes team was to American daguerreotype. Both portraits and views are prized by collectors. *Rare* and *premium*. (Watch for modem prints from the original negatives which are of considerably less value).

Hill, Levi L. United States; 1845-60; daguerreotypes.

New York photographer who produced daguerreotypes in the "colors of nature" in 1850 and was never able to repeat the process. *Rare*; color images *premium*.

Hillers, John K. United States; 1870s; albumen prints, stereographs.

One of a group of photographers who documented expansion into the American West. *Rare*.

Jackson, William Henry. United States; 1860 to 1880s; albumen prints, stereographs.

One of the most famous photographers of the American West, known for his early views of Yellowstone. A number of Western towns and landmarks are named after him. *Rare*.

Johnson and Wolcott. United States/England; 1839-43; daguerreotypes.

John Johnson and Alexander Wolcott opened the first daguerreotype studio in the United States in March 1840, after development of the speculum camera. They were partners with Richard Beard in the first London gallery, opened in October 1840. Despite dedicated contributions to the art, they switched their efforts to other areas in 1844. *Rare* and *premium*.

Käsebier, Gertrude. United States; 1890s; platinum prints.

Opened fashionable portrait studio in New York in 1897. Received "rave reviews" for her artistic, "unadorned" images. Photographed Sioux Indians in 1898. *Rare*.

Kurtz, William. United States; 1870s to 1880s; cabinet cards.

One of a group of very prestigious New York cabinet portrait photographers, Kurtz popularized the use of "Rembrandt" fighting. Portraits of notables *rare*.

Langenheim, William and Frederick. United States; 1842-74; all areas of photography.

Began practicing daguerreotype in Philadelphia in 1842. Became American patent holders for calotype process in 1847. Patented photographs on glass ("hyalotypes") in 1850. Also produced glassstereographs and magic lantern slides. Works identified as Langenheims are *rare* or *uncommon*.

Laurent, Juan. Spain; 1860s to 1870s; albumen prints.

Produced albums and series relating to architecture and landscapes of Spain and Portugal. Also Spanish arms and armor. *Rare*.

Lawrence, Martin. United States; 1844-60; daguerreotypes.

Well-known New York daguerreotypist who specialized in large-plate images. *Rare*.

Le Gray, Gustave. France; 1840s to 1850s; calotypes, albumen prints.

Inventor of the waxed-negative improvement to the calotype. Identified works by Le Gray are *premium*.

Le Secq, Henri. France; 1840-80; calotypes, cyanotypes.

Produced calotypes of Egyptian scenes. *Rare* and *premium*.

MacPherson, Robert. Italy; 1850s to 1860s; albumen prints.

Famous for his views of Roman architecture. *Rare*.

Martin, Paul. England; 1890s; carbon and platinum prints.

British portrait photographer who produced candid street scenes using a concealed camera. *Rare*.

Marville, Charles. France; 1850s; calotypes, albumen prints.

Documented mid-nineteenth century Paris through views of the city, its cathedrals, and its back streets. *Rare*.

Maull and Polyblank. England; 1860s; cartes de visite.

Produced portraits of British notables for mass-distribution and sales. Cartes de visite of important figures *uncommon*.

Mayall, John. United States/England; daguerreotypes, cartes de visite, and stereographs.

This London photographer achieved early notoriety as a superb portraitist. He took excellent daguerreotype views of the Crystal Palace. Early work *rare* and *premium*; other work *uncommon*.

Meade, Charles and Henry. United States; 1842-58; calotypes, daguerreotypes, stereographs.

Two of the most active and influential American daguerreotypists, the Meades visited France in 1848 taking calotypes and daguerreotypes, including some of Daguerre. Most prolific of daguerreotype stereographers. *Rare* and *premium*.

Muybridge, Eadweard. United States, 1856-80; albumen prints, stereographs.

One of a group of photographers documenting expansion to the American West. Later became famous for his photographic studies of animal locomotion, published in several volumes (*premium*). His images of Yosemite and the West, as well as individual motion studies, are *rare*.

Nadar, France; 1850s to 1880s; Albumen prints, cartes de visite, cabinets, salt prints, and carbon prints.

One of the most famous of French photographers, specializing in "character" portraits of celebrities and politicians. Also produced aerial images and photographs by artificial light. His larger prints (including work published in "Galerie Contemporaine") are *rare*; card photographs *uncommon* and *rare*.

Negre, Charles. France; 1850s; calotypes, albumen prints.

Produced a variety of architectural, scenic, and documentary works, including studies of the Midi area of southern France. *Rare*.

North, Walter. United States; 1850-80; daguerreotypes, cartes de visite, cabinets, albumen prints.

An early specialist in negative retouching, North taught and wrote about the subject and received awards in the 1870s. *Rare*.

Notman, William. Canada; 1850s to 1870s; daguerreotypes, albumen prints, platinum prints, stereographs, cartes de visite, cabinets.

Most famous Canadian portrait and landscape photographer. *Rare*; stereographs and cards *uncommon*.

O'Sullivan, Timothy. United States; 1860 to 1880s; albumen prints, cartes de visite, stereographs.

One of the most famous members of Mathew Brady's Photographic Corps, O'Sullivan documented the American Civil War and Westward expansion. Most of his work is *rare*.

Plumbe, John. United States; 1840-48; daguerreotypes.

Maintained the largest chain of galleries in the United States, with branches in England and France. Was the most active early daguerreotypist and supplier. Imprint on brass mat. Many galleries continued to use his name after they were sold to the operators in 1847. Verified work by Plumbe is *rare*; attributed works are *uncommon*.

Ponti, Carlo. Italy; 1858-75; albumen prints.

Produced prints and series of Italian scenery and Roman architecture, also documentary images of Venetian beggars (1860s). Complete albums *premium*; others *rare*.

Quinet, Archille. France; 1870s; albumen prints.

Known for albums and folios of Paris views. *Rare*.

Rehn, Isaac. United States; 1848 to 1860s; daguerreotype and ambrotypes.

Active in the introduction and promotion of the ambrotype process. *Rare*, especially large-plate ambrotypes.

Rejlander, Oscar Gustave. England; 1850s to 1860s; albumen prints.

One of the early leaders in the "art" movement in photography. His "pictorial" images were often staged, using models. *Rare*.

Richards, Frederick De Bourg. United States; 1844-67; daguerreotypes, cartes de visite.

One of the earliest carte de visite photographers in America. Early works *rare*; later cartes de visite *uncommon*.

Riis, Jacob August. United States; 1887 to 1890s; gelatin prints.

Famous for his depictions of immigrant life in New York. Most images which come to market are later reprints from the original negatives. *Rare*.

Robertson, James. England; 1850s; calotypes, albumen prints.

Covered the Crimean War with Fenton. All early documentary images of this type are *rare*.

Robinson, Henry Peach. England; 1850s to 1860s; albumen, platinum, and carbon prints.

With Gustave Rejlander, Robinson was an early promoter of "art" photography, using models and combining negatives to produce somewhat theatrical scenes. *Rare*.

Root, Marcus. United States; 1843 to 1860s; daguerreotypes, ambrotypes, albumen prints, cartes de visite.

Very active and influential daguerreotypist and photographer. Produced microscopic images, used Whipple's innovations (crayon daguerreotypes and crysallotypes from glass negatives), and authored several books on photography. *Rare*.

Russell, A. J. United States; 1860s to 1870s; albumen prints.

The only official military photographer of the Civil War. Produced album documenting military railroads (premium), then was hired by the Union Pacific to document transcontinental construction (1868-69). *Rare*.

Salzmann, Auguste. France; 1850s; calotypes.

Produced studies of Jerusalem to be printed and distributed by Blanquart-Evrard. *Rare*.

Sarony, Napolean. United States; 1860s to 1890s; albumen prints, cartes de visite, cabinets.

Famous for portraits of celebrities and stage performers. Portraits of well-known subjects *rare*; others *uncommon*.

Savage, Charles R. United States; 1859-83; albumen prints, cartes de visite, stereographs.

Famous photographer of the American southwest. Documented the driving of the "golden spike" completing the transcontinental railroad at Promontory, New Mexico (1869). His larger prints are *rare*; some cartes de visite and stereographs are *uncommon*.

Shew family: William, Myron, Jacob, and Trueman. United States; 1841-1900; daguerreotypes, cartes de visite, cabinets, albumen prints.

This family of pioneering photographers and case makers operated galleries in New York, Boston, and Philadelphia, and finally settled in San Francisco (1850s). Cased images *rare*; card photos *common* and *uncommon*.

Silvy, Camille. Britain; 1850s to 1860s; albumen prints, cartes de visite.

Produced startlingly artistic landscape images of England and France, as well as superb portraits. Large prints *rare*; cartes de visite *uncommon*.

Southworth and Hawes. United States; 1840 to 1870s; daguerreotypes, albumen prints.

The team of Josiah Johnson Hawes and Albert Sands Southworth produced some of the most spectacular large-plate daguerreotype images ever made. Their use of lighting and poses to bring out the personality of the sitter was unrivaled, as was their ability to produce unique views and group daguerreotypes. *Rare* and *premium*.

Stieglitz, Alfred. United States; 1880s to 1890s; platinum and carbon prints.

Leader of the Photo-Secessionist movement, Stieglitz was dedicated to producing realistic imagery using natural lighting. Although most of his work was produced after the turn of the century, his early work is prized by collectors. *Premium*.

Stone, John Benjamin. England; 1890s; platinum prints.

Produced extensive study of British peasants and folk festivals. Advocated the use of photography as a record of people, landscapes, and architecture. *Rare*.

Sutcliffe, Frank M. England; 1870s to 1890s; albumen, platinum, carbon, and gelatin prints.

Known for images of the people and landscapes of the seaport of Whitby, England. *Rare*.

Talbot, William Henry Fox. England; 1840s; calotypes.

The inventor of the calotype process. Unfortunately, many of his works have not survived in good condition. *Rare*.

Thomson, John. Scotland; 1860s to 1880s; albumen prints and woodburytypes.

Known for his images of the Far East and for his illustrated books depicting the people of China and the "Street Life in London." *Rare*.

Upton, Benjamin Franklin. United States; 184798; daguerreotypes, albumen prints, and stereographs.

Photographed the Indian settlements in Minnesota and Florida. *Rare*.

Vance, Robert. United States; 1850-60; daguerreotypes.

Provided important early documentation of California and the gold fields. Owned major San Francisco gallery. A large number of his views remain undiscovered. *Rare* and *premium*.

Watkins, Carleton. United States; 1850s to 1880s; daguerreotypes, albumen prints, stereographs.

Photographed the early American West, specializing in California landscapes. *Rare* and *premium*; stereos *uncommon*.

Whipple, John. United States; 1844 to 1880s; daguerreotypes, ambrotypes, albumen prints.

Very active daguerreotypist, inventor, and photographic pioneer. Produced crayon daguerreotypes (vignetted) and early paper photographs from glass negatives called "crystallotypes." Experimented with microphotography and celestial photography. *Rare* and *premium*.

Whitehurst, Jesse. United States; 1842 to 1860s; daguerreotypes, ambrotypes, albumen prints.

While his name is not as well known as that of John Plumbe, Whitehurst was equally involved in promotion and advancement of the art. He owned a large number of galleries along the East Coast and was the recipient of numerous awards. *Rare* and *premium*.

Wolcott, Alexander. United States/England; 1840s; daguerreotypes.

Co-owner of the world's first portrait gallery. Helped Richard Beard develop his chain of London galleries. *Rare* and *premium*.

APPENDIX B

Manufacturers and Their Marks
Daguerreotype Plate Manufacturers

The plate hallmarks shown here were taken from an examination of 200 randomly chosen daguerreotypes. The bold figure in parentheses in the caption accompanying each hallmark indicates the quantity of plates which bore that mark. In addition, 60 plates did not exhibit any evidence of a hallmark and were classified as self-cut plates, and 6 contained partial hallmarks that could not be positively attributed.

Anthony —Edward Anthony & Co., New York City
In addition to the Anthony hallmark plates shown here, this major distributor sold various other French and American-made plates, as well as cases, chemicals, cameras, etc.

Fig. A-1. Edward Anthony & Co. hallmark from the late 1840s (**2**).

Fig. A-2. Edward Anthony & Co. hallmark from approximately 1850 (**1**).

Fig. A-3. Edward Anthony & Co. hallmark from the 1850s; there was no "40" used after 1853 (**2**).

Binsse —Louis B. Binsse & Co., New York City
One of the earliest suppliers of daguerreotype plates and apparatus.

Fig. A-4. Louis B. Binsse & Co. hallmark from the early 1840s (attributed) (**2**).

Fig. A-5. Louis B. Binsse & Co. hallmark from the mid-to-late 1840s (**2**).

L.B. BINSSE & C⁰ N.Y.   40

Christofle —Christofle Scale Plates, France
The first plate manufacturer to produce factory-galvanized plates, starting in the early 1850s.

Fig. A-6. Christofle Scale Plates hallmark (**2**).

Corduan —Joseph Corduan; Corduan, Perkins, & Co., New York
The earliest American plate manufacturer. Plates bearing the Corduan hallmark date from the period 1839 to 1843 and are rare.

Fig. A-7. Corduan, Perkins, & Co. hallmark (**1**).

CORDUAN & Cⁿ N.Y.

French —Benjamin French, Boston, Massachusetts
Primary supplier to Southworth & Hawes in the late 1840s and early 1850s.

Fig. A-8. Benjamin French hallmark (**1**).

Gaudin —A. Gaudin, France
Popular plate used during the early 1850s.

Fig. A-9. A. Gaudin hallmark (**15**).

H.B. plates —France
One of the most popular plates with daguerreotypists throughout the 1850s.
The actual name is unknown.

Fig. A-10. H. B. hallmark (**20**).

Holmes, Booth, & Hayden
(Israel Holmes, John Booth, Henry Hayden); Waterbury, Connecticut, and New York City
One of the largest and most active photographic supply houses in the United States. Began to produce daguerreotype plates in 1853.

Fig. A-11. Holmes, Booth & Hayden hallmark from the mid-1850s (**4**).

Fig. A-12. Holmes, Boot, & Hayden hallmark ("Wreath Plate") from the late 1850s (**6**).

Houssemaine—Unknown European platemaker, late 1840s.
HOUSSEMAINE-GARANTY (**1**)

J.F.S. —France
Popular plate, known among daguerreotypists as the "star" plate. Produced mid-to-late 1850s.

Fig. A-13. J.F.S. hallmark (**8**).

J.P. —France
Very popular French plate produced during the mid-1850s.

Fig. A-14. J.P. hallmark (**20**).

N.P. —France
Another popular French plate produced from 1849 through the 1850s.

Fig. A-15. N.P. hallmark (**5**).

№ 40

Norton —J.W. Norton, New York City
Supplied plates and daguerreotype apparatus during the late 1850s.

Fig. A-16. J. W. Norton hallmark (**2**).

NORTON

Scovills —William and Lamson Scovill, Waterbury, Connecticut
One of the largest distributors of photographic supplies in America, from 1839 into the twentieth century (merged with Anthony & Co. in 1901 to form Ansco).

Fig. A-17. Scovills hallmark from the late 1840s (**18**).

SCOVILLS

Fig. A-18. Scovills hallmark from the early 1840s (**1**).

SCOVILLS №2

Fig. A-19. Scovills hallmark from the 1850s (**8**).

W.H.H. —Unknown American maker of daguerreotype plates popular during late 1840s and early 1850s.

Fig. A-20. W.H.H. hallmark (**3**).

W.H.H.

White —Edward White, New York City
Daguerreotypist, case maker, and supplier who sold his plates through various major distributors throughout the 1840s.

Fig. A-21. Edward White hallmark (**2**).

E. WHITE MAKER NY FINEST QUALITY A No.1

*40 —Unknown French platemaker.
A popular plate from 1848 through the 1850s.

Fig. A-22. Hallmark of an unknown French platemaker (**8**).

APPENDIX C

Collector Resources

ARCHIVAL SUPPLIES

The following are recognized sources for archival tapes, paper, mount board, storage boxes, glues, and more:

Light Impressions
439 Monroe Avenue
P.O. Box 940
Rochester, NY 14603-0940
1-800-828-6216
http://lightimpressionsdirect.com/

University Products, Inc.
P.O. Box 101
Holyoak, MA 01041-0101
1-800-628-1912
http://www.crocker.com/~univ/

Conservation Resources
8000-H Forbes Place
Springfield, VA 22151
1-800-624-6932

BOOK RESOURCES

The following businesses specialize in books related to photo history and collecting:

A Photographers Place
133 Mercer St.
New York, NY 10012
(212) 431-9358

Fred Pajerski
250 W. 24th St. 4GE
New York, NY 10011
(212) 255-6501

ACR Books
8500 La Entrada
Whittier, CA 90605
(310) 693-8421
http://www.webtch.com/ACRbooks/

COLLECTOR CLUBS AND ORGANIZATIONS

The following organizations are composed of image collectors and historians and are an excellent resource for additional information on photo-history and/or collecting trends:

American Photographic .
1150 Avenue of the Americas
New York, NY 10036
(212) 575-0483
http://www.superexpo.com/aphs/

Daguerreian Society
3045 West Liberty Ave., Suite 7
Pittsburgh, PA 15216-240
(412) 343-5525
http://java.austinc.edu/dag

George Eastman House
Joyce Herbert, Membership Manager
900 East Avenue
Rochester, NY 11607
(716) 271-3361; ext. 233
http://www.eastman.org

National Stereoscopic Association
P.O. Box 14801
Columbus, Ohio 43214
http://www.3d-web.com/nsa/nsa.htm

The Photographic Historical Society
P.O. Box 39563
Rochester, NY 14604
http://www.rit.edu/~andpph/tphs.html

IMAGE DEALERS AND AUCTION HOUSES

The following dealers/auction houses provided images for this book and are a good resource for purchasing images of the type shown herein:

Paul Berg
P.O. Box 8895
Newport Beach, CA 92660
(714) 759-3069
Buys and sells cases and wall frames.
Also a source for his book, *Nineteenth Century Photographic Cases & Wall Frames*, and reprints of his articles for the *Daguerreian Annual*.

Etherton Gallery
135 S. 6th Ave.
Tucson, AZ 85701
(520) 624-7370
19th, 20th century and contemporary photographs

Tom Flood, Autographs & Collectibles
P.O. Box 4905
Walnut Creek, CA 94596
(510) 945-1337

Charles Isaacs
2145 Valley Hill Road
Malvern, PA 19355
(610) 827-9500
19th and 20th century photographic masterworks

John & Jelena McWilliams
One Nations Historic Antiques
4555 N. Pershing Ave. #33-370
Stockton, CA 95207
(209) 952-3855
Holds two major image auctions each year with quality catalog.
Also does private/direct sales.

Julie & Dominic Santangelo
P.O. Box 222
Bellingham, WA 98227
1-800-734-3986
Buys and sells fine vintage photographica, early advertising, antique scientific instruments, and historic Americana.

Charles Schwartz, Ltd.
21 E. 90th Street
New York, NY 10128
(212) 534-4496
Dealer in rare and important 19th century photography.
By appointment.

Joseph T. Silva, Fine Americana
P.O. Box 1281
Lafayette, CA 94549-1281
(925) 372-8743

Swann Galleries, Inc., Auctioneers
104 E. 25th Street
New York, NY 10010
(212) 254-4710
Bi-annual auction of photography, including significant 19th century cased and paper images.

APPENDIX D

Electronic Cleaning of Daguerreotypes

Warning: The cleaning of daguerreotypes by other than trained conservators is not recommended. Those who use the following instructions to clean daguerreotypes do so at their own risk. Instructions must be followed to the letter to achieve proper results.

Read the instructions completely through before you begin. Only gilded daguerreotypes can be cleaned in this manner—non-gilded images may be permanently damaged or destroyed. Only a trained technician with proper equipment can determine if an image has been gilded. This process involves the use of pure ammonia—use in a well-ventilated area and protect the skin, eyes, and face from splashing. Purchase only pure ammonia. DO NOT use ammonia-based cleaners or ammonia that contains even the slightest amount of additives, such as soaps or perfumes.

Items needed: Aluminum foil, shallow glass bowl or tray, pure ammonia, and distilled water.

THE PROCESS:

1. Remove the daguerreotype plate from its case and packet as described in Chapter 4. Set the plate aside, face up, in a safe area. Do not touch or allow anything to contact the surface of the plate.

2. Tear off a generous piece of aluminum foil and create a tray with short sides and a base of approximately the same dimensions as the daguerreotype plate. This tray should be well-sealed at the corners so that it is capable of holding liquid.

3. Place this tray into a shallow, flat-bottomed glass bowl or tray and add about 3/8 inch pure ammonia.

4. Holding the plate by its edges over a sink or drain, pour a generous amount of distilled water over the front and back to wash off any fine dust or debris. Carefully shake off the excess water.

5. Carefully place the daguerreotype plate face-up in the tray of ammonia. Gently rock the tray back and forth intermittently. The tarnish may clear quickly—if it does, remove the plate and move immediately to step six. If the tarnish does not clear quickly, continue to gently rock the tray until the plate has cleared or until the aluminum foil has turned a dull gray (oxidized).

6. Carefully remove the plate from the ammonia bath and hold it under flowing warm tap water for several minutes. At some point during the rinse, carefully wipe any residue off the BACK of the plate with a paper towel. Then rinse again under flowing water.

7. Next, rinse the plate well with distilled water. **Note:** It is very important that the final rinse be done with distilled water.

8. Dry the plate. This is very tricky and can be done in a variety of ways. An improperly dried plate will show water spots and/or stains. Carefully shake off as much water as possible, then use either warm sunshine or hold the plate at a distance from radiated heat, such as an electric stove top burner. Flame sources may contain fumes that are detrimental to the image. DO NOT overheat the plate.

9. Once the plate is thoroughly dried, replace the mat and tape it to a new glass as described in Chapter 4.

10. Write the words "electrolytically cleaned" and the date of the cleaning on the seal.

APPENDIX E

Case Makers and Designers

Brady, Mathew (New York City)
Designed and manufactured several cases during the early 1840s, the most valuable of which has the image of a harp in the center and is embossed with the words, "Mathew B. Brady, Casemaker, N.Y."

Chapman, Levi L. (New York City)
Manufactured a number of designs during the early 1850s, including several "bookstyle" cases, some with the Chapman label inside the front cover.

Critchlow, Alfred P. (Florence, Massachusetts)
Began producing plastic cases in 1853. Cases bearing the Critchlow label date from the period 1853 to 1857, at which time the name of the firm became Littlefield, Parsons, & Co. (see Florence Manufacturing Co., below).

Eichmeyer, H. A. (Philadelphia, Pennsylvania)
Famous for designing the "band" case, a bookstyle case with a rounded spine and two embossed bands encircling the case. Many variations were produced by other firms.

Florence Manufacturing Co. (Florence, Massachusetts)
Name used by Littlefield, Parsons, & Co. on plastic cases produced after 1866.

Gaskill & Copper (Philadelphia, Pennsylvania)
Produced papier-mâché cases during the late 1850s; tiny embossed name appears in the motif.

Holmes, Booth, and Hayden (New York City)
Manufactured plastic cases in the late 1850s and after. (See also previous section, "Daguerreotype Plate Manufacturers.")

Littlefield, Parsons, and Co. (Florence, Massachusetts)
Major case manufacturer, successor to Critchlow. Plastic cases with this name on the label date from the period 1858 to 1866.

Loekle, Charles (Philadelphia, Pennsylvania)
Engraver. Some cases, produced during the mid-1850s, have his name embossed in the design.

Paquet, Anthony C. (Philadelphia, Pennsylvania)
Engraver. Embossed his name on case designs during the mid-1850s.

Peck, Samuel (New Haven, Connecticut)
Credited with having designed and produced the first plastic case in 1852. Coined the name "Union case." Partner in Scovill Manufacturing Co. from 1851 to 1857. Peck's name was removed from the Scovill label sometime after 1857.

Plumbe, John (New York City)
Famous daguerreotypist and promoter. Produced wood-frame cases until 1847, often imprinting his name on a label inside. (See also "Nineteenth-Century Photographers of Note.")

Pretlove, David (New York City)
Engraver. Name incorporated into several leather case motifs.

Scovill Manufacturing Co. (New York City)
Produced plastic cases under Peck's patent from 1854 until 1857, at which time Peck's interests were bought out. Production continued into the 1860s. (See also previous section, "Daguerreotype Plate Manufacturers.")

Shew family: Myron, Jacob, and William
(Boston, Massachusetts)
Produced wood-frame cases during mid-to-late 1840s, usually with identifying label in back. Condition of extant cases indicates poor construction methods. (See also "Nineteenth-Century Photographers of Note," Appendix A.)

Smith, J. (New York City)
Engraver. Name incorporated into motifs of plastic cases during late 1850s.

GLOSSARY

Definitions are also provided for terms appearing in *italic* in the descriptions.

accessories: Items in a photograph other than the sitter; e.g., canes, cigars, hats, chairs, pedestals, drapery, etc. See also *furnishings*.

album: A group of pages bound together like a book designed to contain photographs. Albums of the nineteenth century were enclosed in fancy leather or velvet covers.

albumen: The white of a chicken egg, used in photography as a base for holding light sensitive silver solutions to paper or glass.

allegorical photograph: A "staged" photograph depicting a story or event with a deeper, underlying meaning. Also referred to as *genre* photographs.

ambrotype: A photographic process in which a negative image is formed on collodion-coated glass, then viewed as positive by the inclusion of a black background.

aristotype: Popular brand name for presensitized *chloride printing-out paper* of the late 1890s.

attributed credit: Credit for an image given to a particular photographer due to the specific characteristics of that image when no concrete evidence is available to verify the photographer. He or she is "assumed" to be the photographer.

balsa gum: A sticky sap collected from balsa wood, used as an adhesive during the nineteenth century. It was used in the Cutting patented ambrotype process to seal a protective cover glass to the image.

bevels: A daguerreotype plate *configuration* consisting of bends along the edge of certain plates, done to make the plate easier to handle during the polishing process.

blindstamp: The photographer's name or logo, embossed into a paper photograph for identification.

boudoir print: A variation of the cabinet card, measuring 8-1/4" x 5", popular from the late 1870s.

bromide print: A photograph made on gelatin-coated silver-bromide paper, the first true "printing" paper, which required development to bring out the *latent image*.

burnished: Given a high-gloss by running the photographic print between hot rollers. An integral part of the *cabinet card* process in later years.

cabinet card: A photographic print mounted to a card measuring 44-1/4" x 62", popular from the late 1860s. Most cabinet cards were albumen prints, although other processes were sometimes used.

calotype: The first practical form of photography on paper, introduced in 1841 as an improvement of Fox Talbot's *photogenic drawing* and *talbotype*.

carbon print: The first "permanent" type of photographic print, patented in 1855 and perfected in 1866. The negative was printed onto carbon tissue, then double-transferred to paper. An expensive and elaborate process, it was usually reserved for exhibition prints.

carte de visite: An albumen print on a lightweight cardboard mount measuring 2-1/2" x 4-1/4", popular from the mid-1850s in Europe and from 1860 in America.

cased image: Any of a group of photographic images contained in a leather, paper, or plastic case, popular from 1839 to about 1867.

ceramic photograph: A collodion-based image which has been transferred to chinaware or porcelain then covered with a ceramic glaze. This is an unusual and expensive photographic variant.

chloride print: A photographic image produced on gelatin-coated silver-chloride *printing-out paper*, which replaced albumen paper near the turn of the century.

chocolate tin: A photographic image produced on lightweight iron plates coated with brown varnish (a variant of the *tintype* or *ferrotype*).

collodion: A highly flammable, viscous pale yellow liquid solution of nitro cellulous, alcohol, and ether. Originally used as a liquid bandage by the military, collodion was found to be the perfect base for holding sensitizing solutions to glass in a photographic process which came to be known as the *wet process*.

combination print: A photographic image produced by printing several different negatives onto one print to produce the desired effect. This technique was often used by art photographers such as Rejlander and Robinson.

configurations: The various marks left on daguerreotype plates by tools and techniques of the process, including *bevels*, *plate holders*, and *gilding* tools.

coral glass: A dark, violet-colored glass used as a base for ambrotypes as a way of eliminating the need for a black backing (also known as *ruby glass*).

crayon daguerreotypes: A vignetted daguerreotype image, patented by John Whipple in 1849, produced by the manipulation of screens behind and in front of the sitter. Crayon daguerreotypes are easier to view, due to a substantial decrease in shadow (reflective) areas.

crystallotype: The first albumen prints from glass negatives produced in America by John Whipple, in 1853.

cyanotype: Also known as "blue prints" or the "ferro-prussiate process." A photographic image consisting of blue lines on a white backround (or vice-versa) developed by Sir John Herschel (1842) and improved by Pellet in 1871. A forerunner of the modern blueprint process.

daguerreotype: The world's first practical photographic process, announced by Frenchman Jacques-Louis-Mande Daguerre in 1839. Daguerretypes were produced on silver-coated copper plates and usually housed in protective leather or plastic cases.

death portrait: See *postmortem*.

documentation: Specific written information about a collectible image, e.g., photographer, process, sitter's name, or plate configurations. Documentation helps to avoid handling of the image by prospective buyers or future owners.

dry plate: A gelatin-based glass plate purchased presensitized from the manufacturer for exposure at the photographer's leisure. Rep laced the collodion wet plate at the turn of the century.

elements: The specific items which make up a *cased image*, which include the *plate, mat, preserver*, case, and cover glass.

emulsion: The light-sensitive coating applied to photographic plates, film, or paper. (**Note:** Among most photohistorians and collectors, this term is usually applied only to gelatin-based coatings.)

estimate: An auction term indicating the price a presented item is expected to bring, usually given as a range (e.g., $200-$350).

ethnics: A collector's term indicating images in which the sitter is of an unusual ethnic background for photographs of the period (e.g., blacks, Indians, Orientals, etc.).

ferrotype: A tintype plate produced by Victor Griswold to compete with Peter Neff's *melainotype* plate in the late 1850s. The term is technically more accurate than *tintype* since the plates were made of iron, not tin.

flat plate: A daguerreotype plate which has no bevels or plate holder *configurations*, usually indicating that the plate was produced during the early years of the process.

folio: A group or *series* of mounted photographs presenting the work of one or more photographers, usually containing the artist's imprint or signature.

foxing: Small brown spots which have developed on older paper photographs, particularly albumen prints, probably caused by chemical instabilities in the paper.

furnishings: Items which make up the setting for a studio portrait, such as chairs, pedestals, drapery, etc.

gallery: Popular name for early portrait studios. Many photohistorians and collectors use the word *gallery* only when referring to *daguerreotype* establishments and the word *studio* for all other photographic establishments.

galvanize: To add additional silver to a daguerreotype plate by electrolysis, thereby improving the quality. Plates which have silver on the back have been galvanized.

gaslight paper: A nickname given to certain gelatin-chloride printing papers which could be developed by artificial light.

gelatin: A clear, tasteless substance made by boiling the bones and skins of animals. Used as base for photographic films and plates since the 1880s.

gelatin dry plate: See *dry plate.*

gelatin print: Although gelatin was used as the base for many photographic processes, this term is usually used in reference to *bromide prints* and *chloride prints.*

gem: A tiny tintype format, approximately 3/4" x 1", produced in a multi-lens camera with a *repeating back.* Gem tintypes were displayed in tiny *albums* or placed in *sleeves.*

genre photographs: A term often used as a synonym for *allegorical photographs*; also describes any image which has a specific theme.

glass positive: A positive photographic image produced by printing the negative directly onto sensitized glass (for viewing by transmitted light).

gold chloride: A solution introduced by Hippolyte Fizeau in 1840 to intensify and protect the finished daguerreotype (see *gilding*). Later gold chloride was used to produce warm tones in cold-tone papers such as albumen.

gravure: See *photogravure.*

gilding: The process of intensifying and toning a daguerreotype image through the application of *gold chloride.*

gilt: In early photography, a small amount of gold applied to the image surface to represent jewelry, buttons, etc.; also, gold applied to cases or mounts as decorative trim.

Gutta-percha: A name incorrectly applied to the plastic substance used to produce the *union case.* Gutta-percha is a pliable sap collected from an Indian tree (called "Inosandra gutta") and used to produce buttons, jewelry, caneheads, etc. Its fragility made it unsuitable for use in the production of photographic cases. See also *union case.*

halftone: A printing process which by converting a photographic image into tiny dots allowed the mechanical reproduction of photographs in books and newspapers; used from the 1880s.

hallmark: The logo or symbol embossed near the edge of a daguerreotype plate as the "signature" of the plate manufacturer. See also *plate mark.*

halo: The area of tarnish on extant daguerreotypes which follows the shape of the mat, surrounding the subject. Halo is considered an "adornment" by some, a distraction by others.

heliograph: The name given by Niepce to the first photographic images, taken on pewter plates in 1827.

heliotype: A "cover term" which includes all of the early processes of Fox Talbot: *photogenic drawings, talbotypes, calotypes*, and "sun pictures." (The term is not commonly used today.)

hyalotype: A positive image printed on glass, used for *stereographs* and *lantern slides*, patented by the Langenheims in 1850.

hypo: Hyposulfate of soda, a solution introduced by Sir John Herschel in 1839 which "fixed" the photographic image, making it insusceptible to the further actions of light. Hypo was used in nearly every major process of the nineteenth century.

imperial carte: A carte de visite on which the portrait image filled as much of the available area as possible (a nineteenth-century "head shot").

imperial photograph: A term used by Mathew Brady to describe his large albumen prints (up to 17" x 20").

imperial print: A large card photograph measuring 7" x 10", popular from the 1880s.

itinerant: A traveling photographer who temporarily set up shop in small towns and communities; during the American Civil War, itinerants visited encampments and battlefields.

Japan varnish: A deep black varnish used to coat *tintype* plates and as a finish for cases (often inlaid with mother-of-pearl).

lantern slide: A transparent glass slide containing a positive photographic image which is projected onto a wall or screen by the light of a *magic lantern.*

latent image: The invisible image which exists on exposed photographic plates or sensitized paper and which can only be brought out by chemical development.

Linked Ring: An organization of photographers who in 1893 broke away from the Royal Photographic Society due to the lack of attention given to "art" photography. Included Henry Peach Robinson as co-founder.

magic background: A vignetting process introduced by Charles Anthony in 1851 employing a series of paper cutouts which, when placed in front of the plate during the exposure, created a halo of light from behind the subject.

magic lantern: A device for the projection of glass slides, incorporating an enlarging lens and the magnified light of a burning flame.

mammoth plates and prints: Images (18" x 22") produced by the giant wet-plate cameras often carried by photographers who documented expansion to the American west.

mascher viewer: A daguerreotype case designed to hold stereographic plates, incorporating a pop-up viewer inside the cover.

mat: A sheet of paper, cardboard, or metal with the center cut out in a particular shape; used to surround, beautify, and protect the image in a cased photograph.

measles: Small spots on a daguerreotype plate, probably caused by residual polishing chemicals. These spots often appear on *renewed* plates, as a reaction to the cleaning solution.

melainotype: The original name for the tintype process as patented by Peter Neff in 1854; it was replaced by the term *ferrotype* in the 1860s.

metol: Metol-hydrochinon solution; used as a developer for bromide and chloride prints near the turn of the century.

mezzotint: A mechanically produced print made from engraved copper plates.

mourning mat: A black paper mat used on daguerreotype images to indicate that the subject had died or was in mourning for someone who had died (see next entry).

mourning portrait: A portrait of a person who is in mourning for a recently deceased friend or relative, sometimes sent to the immediate family of the dead person when the sitter could not be there in person.

nonpariel: A French term meaning "unparalleled" or "without equal." The term was a freely used catch-word in Victorian times but was used in photography to designate a specific shape of mat that incorporated a French curve in its design.

opaltype: A positive image on white milk glass, coated with a gelatin-bromide emulsion; a cheaper, easier-to-make version of *ceramic photographs*.

Oreo case: See *sweetheart case*.

original print: A photographic print made from the original negative by the original photographer or his authorized agent.

orotone: A positive image on glass, backed with gold foil.

oxidation: A film which appears on metal-based images as a result of chemical reactions with the air or moisture.

panel print: One of the odd-sized card photographs produced during the late nineteenth century, this one 4" x 8-1/4".

Passe-partout: A framing style consisting of a painted, pressed cardboard mat sealed to a cover-glass (sometimes also painted); preferred by Europeans for daguerreotypes and ambrotypes.

Photo-Secession group: A society formed by Alfred Stieglitz during the early twentieth century for the promotion of "pictorial" photography. Gertrude Kasebier and Edward Steichen were also co-founders.

photogenic drawing: The earliest images produced by Fox Talbot, in which leaves or lace were placed in contact with salted paper and exposed in the sun, resulting in a contact negative.

photograph: In the early years of the art, a term applied only to those images produced on paper; later, a more general designation for any image produced by the action of light.

photogravure: A high-quality photomechanical reproduction printed from engraved copper plates. (See Fig. 8-4.)

pinhole photography: Discovered by John Mascher in 1855; refers to a process in which a sensitized plate is placed in an enclosed box with a small hole opposite it, an image of the object or scene in front of the hole is produced on the plate.

pirated photograph: An image (usually a portrait of a celebrity) that was taken by one photographer and copied and sold by another without permission. For obvious reasons, pirated photographs are seldom imprinted with a logo.

plate mark: The name or *hallmark* of a platemaker which is embossed near the edge of a daguerreotype plate.

platinum print: A photographic image on paper, formed entirely by precipitated platinum. One of the most permanent types of photographs.

plumbeotype: An engraved mechanical print produced from a daguerreotype original. The process was popularized by John Plumbe in the late 1840s. It is not a photographic process.

porcelain print: A positive photographic image produced by printing the negative directly onto sensitized porcelain.

portfolio: See *folio*.

postmortem: A portrait of a deceased person, taken to give the appearance that the person is sleeping. Common during the period of the *cased image*; less common in later years.

preserver: A thin frame of malleable brass which encompasses the *plate mat* and the cover-glass of a *cased image*, holding them securely in place.

Printing-out paper: Photographic paper which produces an image during exposure and does not require chemical development (*albumen* paper, *aristotype* paper, etc.).

promenade print: One of a variety of card photographs produced during the late nineteenth century; this one measures 3-3/4" x 7-1/2".

provenance: The history of a photograph, including (when possible) its place of origin and all of its previous owners.

quickstuff: A chemical mixture (often a secret formula of the operator) that was applied to a daguerreotype plate via a "fuming box" to increase sensitivity.

renewed plate: A daguerreotype plate which has been cleaned with a chemical dip to remove tarnish. Renewal of daguerreotype plates is not recommended.

repeating back: An attachment to a wet-plate camera which allowed the separate exposure of each half of the plate. Used in combination with a multi-lens setup, the repeating back allowed for the production of dozens of images on one plate.

reserve: An auction term signifying the lowest amount the seller will take for a particular item.

rub: A blemish in a daguerreotype image caused by contact with the surface of the plate.

ruby glass: See *coral glass*.

salt print: A print made on *calotype* paper from a glass negative.

salting: Small green spots on daguerreotype plates and brass mats caused by a chemical reaction to air and moisture.

self-cut plate: A plate cut by the operator from a larger plate to save money. Plates without *plate marks* have usually been self-cut.

series: A group of photographs pertaining to the same subject, usually distributed as a set.

shield: A light-tight holder into which a photographic plate is inserted for transportation to the camera. After it is placed into the camera, a slide is removed, allowing the plate to be exposed.

shorted plate: A *self-cut plate* made slightly smaller than standard size. By this method a "thrifty" operator could get more plates for his money.

silver bromide, silver chloride, silver nitrate: The three major sensitizing solutions used in the nineteenth century.

silver print: A generic name given to all paper prints produced after the introduction of gelatin-coated paper, on which the image is formed by silver.

silvering: The silver "dusting" which occurs near the edges of aging gelatin prints.

sleeve: A carte de visite-sized paper frame into which a *tintype* or *gem* tintype was inserted for protection and adornment.

solarization: A brilliant white area on a daguerreotype, containing little or no detail, caused by overexposure of light-colored objects. This was a common problem during the early years of the process and prompted operators to insist that the sitter wear clothing of a neutral shade.

speculum camera: A type of camera invented by Wolcott and Johnson (1839 to 1840). Rather than a lens, the camera used a concave metal reflector which projected the image onto a sensitized daguerreotype plate. The shorter exposure times required by this camera made portraiture possible and inspired the first commercial studio.

stereograph: A pair of pictures of the same object, taken at slightly different angles, presented side by side for viewing in a *stereoscope*.

stereoscope: A binocular device for viewing stereoscopic pictures. The spacing and angle provided by special lenses produces a three-dimensional effect.

sweetheart case: A type of *union case* consisting of two discs which are attached together by screw-threads or friction, with one or both discs holding the round image. Because of their resemblance to a popular modem cookie, these cases have obtained the nickname *Oreo case*.

talbotype: A photographic image produced on salted paper by continued exposure in a camera. This process was the predecessor to the *calotype* process, in which the *latent image* was brought out through chemical development.

third foot: Nickname for the infamous head rest used to hold the sitter's head steady during lengthy exposures. In standing portraits, the base of the support is often seen next to the subject's feet, inspiring the nickname "third foot."

tintype: Popular misnomer for the *melainotype* and *ferrotype* process; tintype images were actually produced on thin sheets of *iron* painted with *Japan varnish*. While the period of the tintype's popularity was short-lived (1858 to 1865), the tintype has the distinction of having been produced in quantity longer than any other nineteenth-century process (1858 to 1930).

Tipped-in: Mounted to a book page or leaf of an album. Books illustrated with original photographs usually have the images tipped-in.

toning: The overall tinting of an image, usually through a bath in *gold chloride*. Toning brings a warmer color to the image and has protective qualities as well.

union case: A type of molded plastic image case, introduced in the early 1850s. The plastic was made by combining wood fibers or coal dust with shellac and color. Incorrectly called the *gutta-percha* case.

Velox: Brand name for a popular *gaslight paper* of the late 1890s.

vignette: A style of portrait in which the image seems to float on a background of light or clouds, produced by various mechanical, optical, or chemical means.

waxed negative: An improvement to the *calotype* process in which the paper negative was coated in wax, thereby making it more transparent.

wet process: Name given to the process in which a negative image was produced on a *collodion*-coated glass plate. In order to assure maximum sensitivity, the plate had to be exposed while still wet.

wiped plate: A daguerreotype plate which has had the image destroyed by attempted cleaning with a cloth or with abrasives.

woodburytype: A elaborate photomechanical printing process popular for illustrated books and *folios*. The image was formed by pigmented gelatin, pressed onto paper by a lead mold.

BIBLIOGRAPHY

This book has provided much of the basic information collectors need to enjoy collecting as a hobby and/or to make wise investment decisions. However, the scope of nineteenth-century photography is far greater than any one volume can even touch on. The serious collector would be well advised to expand his or her education through continued reading. What follows is a list of the best-known books dealing with the various aspects of this subject, each accompanied by a simple review. Please keep in mind that some of these books are now out of print, but should be available through interlibrary loan, or for purchase through used-book search services. Otherwise, most of the books listed are available from the dealers listed in the Collector's Resources appendix.

Albumen and Salted Paper Book, by James M. Redly (Light Impressions, Rochester, NY, 1980).

A comprehensive guide to the history and technique of albumen printing, with emphasis on the process itself.

The American Daguerreotype, by Floyd and Marion Rinhart (University of Georgia Press, Athens, Georgia, 1981).

A "must have" for daguerreotype collectors, this large volume is the most comprehensive study available to date. Extensive appendix and biographical sections.

American Miniature Case Art, by Floyd and Marion Rinhart (A.S. Bames and Co., Cranbury, New Jersey, 1969).

While the recent Krainik book *Union Cases* (presented later), covers that specific type of case thoroughly, the Rinharts' book is still the only comprehensive volume covering all aspects of image case history and production.

Art of the Daguerreotype, by Setfan Richter, with an Introduction by Helmut Gernsheim, (Viking, London, England, 1989)

Lavishly illustrated with primarily European images, this volume contains marvelous examples of fully colored daguerreotypes, as well as art nudes and erotica.

Care and Identification of 19th Century Photographic Prints, by James M. Reilly (Eastman Kodak Co., 1986).

One of the most thorough books on the subject, this volume contains color plates, closeup illustrations, and a wall chart.

Cartes de Visite in 19th Century Photography, by William Darrah (self-published, Gettysburg, Pennsylvania, 1981).

A very extensive technical history of the carte; includes thorough subject guide and large photographer index.

Collecting Photographica, by George Gilbert (Hawthorne Books, New York, New York, 1976).

Outdated but still interesting reading.

Daguerreotype: A Sesquicentennial Celebration, edited by John Wood (University of Iowa Press, Iowa City, Iowa, 1989).

An impressive volume containing many previously unpublished images and informative essays by noted authorities.

The Daguerreotype in America, by Beaumont Newhall (Dover Publications, New York, New York, 1976).

Authoritative information from a leading photo historian. Not as complete as the Rinhart book, but a good inexpensive substitute with some excellent plates.

Daguerreotypes of Southworth and Hawes, by Robert Sobieszek and Odette Appel (Dover Publications, New York, New York, 1980).

More than 100 plates by two of the most artistic and prolific American daguerreotypists; each plate has accompanying text.

Dictionary of American Portraits

Once out-of-print collection of more than 4,000 famous people from history. The perfect answer to the common question, "Doesn't this guy look like somebody important?" A pricey but invaluable reference.

Dressed for the Photographer: Ordinary Americans & Fashion, by Joan Severa.

An excellent resource for dating images by clothing styles.

French Daguerreotypes, by Janet Buerger.

A scholarly and wonderfully illustrated volume. A "must have" for collectors of European images.

George Eastman: A Biography, by Elizabeth Brayer.

Well-researched history of the man who brought photography to the masses.

Golden Age of British Photography (1839-1900), by Mark Haworth-Booth (Aperture, New York, New York, 1984).

A superb portfolio of images from the top museums in Great Britain, with informative text.

History of Photography, by Helmut and Alison Gernsheim (London, Thames, and Hudson, 1969).

An early, but still authoritative history.

History of Photography, by Beaumont Newhall (Museum of Modern Art, New York, New York, 1982).

A "must have" for image collectors; covers the processes and "trends" from the beginning of the art into the twentieth century. An excellent reference work.

How to Buy Photographs, by Stuart Bennett (Phaidon Press, Oxford, England, 1987).

Concentrates primarily on "high-end" art photography from the turn of the century; touches lightly on early works and has a section on modern prints. European flavor.

International Guide to 19th Century Photographers, by Gary Edwards (G. K. Hall, 1988).

Lists more than 4,000 names with pertinent information, including auction catalog listings.

Keepers of Light, by William Crawford (Morgan and Morgan, Dobbs Ferry, New York, 1979).

An extensive guidebook to early photographic processes, with emphasis on chemicals, materials, and techniques.

L.J.M. Daguerre, by Helmut and Alison Gemsheim (Dover Publications, New York, New York, 1968).

First published in 1956, this work is still the authoritative source for information on the inventor of the world's first practical photographic process. Numerous related plates.

Military Uniforms in America: Long Endure: The Civil War Period, edited by John Elting and Michael McAfee (Presidio Press, Novato, California, 1982).

Complete reference of "standard" military uniforms for the period 1852 to 1867. Important to collectors of military images.

Mr. Lincoln's Camera Man, Mathew Brady, by Roy Meredith (Dover Publications, New York, New York, 1974).

Complete study of the life and work of America's most famous nineteenth-century photographer. Contains examples of his early works, as well as Civil War and postwar images.

Nineteenth Century Photographic Cases and Wall Frames, by Paul Berg.

The most thorough examination of the variety of photographic cases assembled to date. A standard reference used by dealers and auction houses.

Origins of Photography, by Helmut Gemsheim (Thames-Hudson, London, England, 1983).

An extensive history of photography's earliest years, superbly illustrated using special printing processes.

Paper & Light, by Richard Brettell (David R. Godine Publisher, Boston, Massachusetts, 1984).

A major survey of the calotype process in France and Great Britain, superbly illustrated.

Photographic History of the Civil War, in five double volumes (Blue and Grey Press, Secaucus, New Jersey, 1987).

The most extensive collection of Civil War photographs ever accumulated; originally published in 1911.

Photographs: A Collector's Guide, by Richard Blodgett (Ballantine Books, New York, New York, 1979).

Concentrates primarily on "high-end" and art photographs usually sold at auction. Prices now outdated.

Photography and the American Scene, by Robert Taft (Dover Publications, New York, New York, 1964).

Originally published in 1938, this work was the earliest extensive photographic history published and is still a required reference for collectors and photo-historians.

Photography: The Early Years, by George Gilbert (Harper and Row, New York, New York, 1980).

A compendium of nineteenth-century photographic history spotlighting famous individual photographers.

Photography: Essays and Images, edited by Beaumont Newhall (Museum of Modern Art, New York, New York, 1980).

Works by and about those individuals who shaped the photographic art. Excellent plates.

Scenic Daguerreotype: Romanticism & Early Photography, by John Wood.

Superbly illustrated book on daguerreotype views.

Union Cases, by Clifford and Michele Krainik (Centennial Photo Service; Grantsburg, Wisconsin, 1988).

An authoritative cataloging of plastic image. A standard reference used by dealers and auction houses.

Victorian and Edwardian Fashion, by Alison Gernsheim (Dover Publications, New York, New York, 1981).

History of fashion taken from original photographs, of which numerous plates are included. An important reference for dating early images.

World of Stereographs, by William Darrah (self-published, Gettysburg, Pennsylvania, 1977).

A complete history of the stereograph, including extensive subject guide and list of stereographers

INDEX

HERE IS A GUIDE FOR YOU...NO MATTER WHAT YOU COLLECT

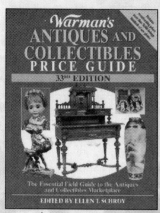

Warman's Antiques and Collectibles Price Guide
33rd Edition
by Ellen T. Schroy
Discover the hottest antiques and collectibles in today's marketplace with this new edition of a popular bestseller, which offers you more than 500 categories, over 50,000 updated price listings, and hundreds of photos. You get the facts and figures on individual collectibles, along with collecting advice, history, tips for spotting reproductions, collectors' clubs, museums, auction houses, and a list of reference books and periodicals relating to each category. Expert advisors also share insider pricing information not available anywhere else.
Softcover • 8-1/4 x 10-7/8 • 640 pages • 600+
WAC33 • $16.95

1999 Price Guide to Limited Edition Collectibles
4th Edition
Edited by Mary Sieber
This is the definitive guide you need to enjoy and evaluate your precious limited edition collectibles. More than 59,000 items-all organized by category and alphabetized by company name. Introductions are written by recognized collectible experts and all values have been reviewed and approved by a panel of secondary market professionals. Listings include the item, issue year, producer, artist name, edition limit, series name and current value.
Softcover • 6 x 9 • 896 pages
200 b&w photos • 40 color photos
LEP04 • $17.95

Campbell's Soup Collectibles from A to Z: A Price and Identification Guide
by David and Micki Young
Mmm, mmm, good! That's what Campbell's Soup collectibles are. This first-ever guide to Campbell's Soup collectibles will be a yummy addition to your collectibles books library. It has color photos and more than 1,200 individual listings with current prices. It's literally the alphabet soup to Campbell's collectibles.
Softcover • 8-1/2 x 11 • 160 pages
400+ color photos
SOUP • $17.95

Cookbooks Worth Collecting
by Mary Barile
Savor our country's heritage with this tasteful book on Early American, 19th- and 20th-century cookbooks, leaflets, brochures, and charity cookbooks. Hundreds of photos with prices and tidbits of history create a recipe for nostalgic and charming reading.
Softcover • 6 x 9 • 240 pages
COOK • $17.95

300 Years of Kitchen Collectibles
Identification & Value Guide, 4th Edition
by Linda Campbell Franklin
Whether you collect things that dice, measure, filter or whir, if they belong in the kitchen you'll find them in this guide to three centuries of domestic tools of trade and offers healthy servings of classic recipes, helpful hints, and fascinating tidbits from 18th , 19th, and 20th century trade catalogs and advertisements. More than 7,000 antique items are arranged by function, from preparation and cooking to housekeeping and gardening, and then valued.
Softcover • 8-1/2 x 11 • 648 pages • 1600 illustrations
KIT04 • $24.95

Hake's Guide to Advertising Collectibles
by Ted Hake
More than 1,500 items are pictured, described and priced in this unique addition to your collectibles library. Items issued by 100 famous American companies from the 1880's to the present are highlighted.
Softcover • 7 x 10 • 192 pages
8-page color section
HGADC • $17.95